MAESTRO

CARL DAVIS: MAESTRO

WENDY THOMPSON

FABER **ff** MUSIC

For Sara

First published in 2016 by Faber Music Ltd
Bloomsbury House, 74–77 Great Russell Street, London WC1B 3DA

Text design by Agnesi Text, Hadleigh, Suffolk
Cover design by Chloë Alexander
Cover photography by Ben Wright
(www.benwrightphotography.com)
Printed and bound in England
by TJ International Ltd, Padstow, Cornwall

ISBN10: 0-571-53958-0
EAN13: 978-0-571-53958-1

To buy Faber Music publications or to find out about the full range of titles
available please contact your local music retailer or Faber Music sales enquiries:
Faber Music Ltd, Burnt Mill, Elizabeth Way, Harlow CM20 2HX
Tel: +44 (0) 1279 82 89 82 Fax: +44 (0) 1279 82 89 83
sales@fabermusic.com   fabermusicstore.com

CONTENTS

OVERTURE

Islington, London. A dank, dark afternoon in early December, 2015. The shops are bright with Christmas lights; people are hurrying quickly to and from the tube station to get out of the persistent drizzle. In a recording studio just off Upper Street, members of the Philharmonia Orchestra are sitting quietly, headphones on, preparing to start the 14th of 16 sessions recording over five and a half hours of music written to accompany one of the most enigmatic classics of the silent film era – Abel Gance's monumental *Napoléon*. Chris Egan, a highly experienced producer from the world of pop music and West End musicals, sits in the control room, directing operations. This is his first experience of working with a more classical orchestral score, but there's no doubting the acuity of his ear. Time is money in the recording world, and everyone works to precise deadlines. On this project, he is working with the conductor and composer Carl Davis, one of the most respected figures in the film, TV and theatre worlds, and the creator of 'Live Cinema' – concert performances of his scores accompanying the screenings of silent films. These are in huge demand all over the world. In October 2016, Davis will celebrate his 80th birthday, and the event will be marked by the simultaneous release on DVD, Blu-Ray and CD of a newly restored, digitally cleaned-up version of *Napoléon*, the score that represents one of his most notable achievements.

This afternoon they will record just 15 minutes' worth of music, in the course of a three-hour session. The section covers a scene in Bonaparte's native island of Corsica, where the young army lieutenant, played by Albert Dieudonné, is outside an inn facing down a mob of surly and unappreciative peasants who would like to see him dead. Dieudonné dominates the small studio screen, a mesmeric presence. He acts with his extraordinary eyes, commanding authority. 'No . . . Our fatherland is France . . . with me!' reads the on-screen text box. The session begins. Davis counts in the click track. The orchestra plays the majestic 'Eagle of Destiny' theme, representing Napoleon's ambition for himself and his country, and then segues into a lively tarantella. 'Cut,' says Egan. He queries a missing note in the second oboe's part. Carl Davis confirms that it should indeed be present. The second oboist says that the note is missing from her part. It is restored, and another take begins. Egan queries the dynamic level of the trombones. The trombones agree to delay a *crescendo* by a second or two. Throughout the afternoon, work proceeds apparently at a snail's pace, with minute attention to detail. Even working with a highly professional band like the Philharmonia, Egan and Davis have to be satisfied that every tiny section of music is absolutely perfect and will synchronise with the images on the screen. Every section is taken, and retaken, and taken again, until that perfection is finally achieved. The session comes to an end; instruments are packed away, and Davis and Egan pore over the results on playback. Two more sessions to go, and this unbelievably ambitious project – for many years an impossible dream – will be on the road to fulfilment.

I
FROM THE BEGINNING

The premiere of *Napoléon* on 30 November 1980 at the Empire Cinema in Leicester Square marked a watershed in Carl Davis's life and career. It was his first major appearance on the podium, and since then his career has run along the dual paths of conductor and composer. For more than half a century this mercurial New Yorker, with his 'can-do' attitude, quick wit and ironic smile, has occupied a unique place in British musical life. Able to produce scores at lightning speed and eager to collaborate with impresarios, choreographers, film directors and orchestras, he works in an impressive range of musical genres. If one avenue shows signs of drying up – always a risk in the commercial world – he simply turns his hand to another, often working on several projects simultaneously. His award-winning film, TV and ballet scores are internationally praised for their brilliance in capturing the mood of a scene, a character, or a fleeting moment. He has played an integral role in the reappraisal of masterpieces from the silent film era, and their performance with newly composed orchestral scores. Orchestras – notoriously surly about their conductors – appreciate his down-to-earth attitude, while his inclusive, unashamedly populist approach to concert programming, which springs from a burning passion for communication, continues to break down the cultural barriers that surround classical music, whether in matters of repertoire or concert-hall etiquette.

Napoléon brought together Carl Davis's past and future. His cultural education as a child growing up in New York City in the

1940s was all-inclusive. He was equally fascinated by opera – as a teenager he stood to watch performances at the Metropolitan Opera House – as by musicals, especially the works of Rodgers and Hammerstein, Lerner and Loewe and Frank Loesser's *Guys and Dolls*. New York was enjoying a huge renaissance in dance, with classical ballet productions at Balanchine's New York City Ballet and the American Ballet Theatre, the tail end of the Ballet Russe de Monte Carlo, and new works from the legendary Martha Graham, doyenne of contemporary dance. There were movie houses all over New York, showing both American and European films. And there was a great deal of music on the radio – both on the classical music station owned by the *New York Times*, and on the New York City station, which broadcast 24 hours a day. Davis says he heard a huge amount of music, and responded eagerly to the stimulus.

His role model was Leonard Bernstein. 'Bernstein was the big success story of my youth. His first musical, *On the Town*, was the first I ever saw, when I was ten. I listened on the radio to his amazing orchestral breakthrough at the New York Philharmonic, when Bruno Walter fell ill and Bernstein took over at the last minute. He conducted classical, he played jazz, he wrote musicals. His lifestyle was so glamorous, he swanned around the world, but it wasn't so much the sensational aspect of him that appealed to me as the idea that one could work in different media and different styles, and excel in all of them.'

Carl Davis was born in Brooklyn on 28 October 1936, to second-generation immigrant Jewish parents. His grandparents on both sides had been part of the diaspora, the dispersal of Jewish communities from the Russian Pale, the western fringes of the vast Russian Empire, now parts of Ukraine, Poland, Belarus and Lithuania. These close-knit communities were fragmented in the late nineteenth and early twentieth centuries by anti-Semitic discrimination – especially the infamous 'May Laws' passed in 1882, that placed severe restrictions on where Jews could live and how they could earn a living, reinforced by sporadic state-authorised violence against them. Some fled to England, many more to America. Between 1880 and 1914 around 1.4 million Russian and Polish Jews sought a new life on the other side of the Atlantic. Over one million settled in New York, where by 1910 they comprised a quarter of the city's population. Many worked either as entrepreneurs or in the clothing industry, but they were ambitious and industrious, well suited to the go-getting dynamic of the New World.

Carl Davis's mother's side of the family was musical. His maternal grandfather, Morris Perlmutter, had been cantor at a synagogue in his Polish home-town of Vilnius (now in Lithuania). Perlmutter was a relatively common Jewish name, but the family may have been related to that of the celebrated pianist Vlado Perlemuter, who was born in Kovno (now Kaunas in Lithuania, about a hundred kilometres from Vilnius) in 1904. Carl's mother recalled that one night, during one of the pianist's rare visits to the USA, he unexpectedly dropped in on the family and played for them. Perlemuter, who spent most of his life in France and Switzerland, was fascinated by English literature, especially Shakespeare and Dickens – a passion shared by the Davis family, whose library was well stocked with the English classics.

Morris Perlmutter left Poland in 1905, on the outbreak of the Russo-Japanese war. He had been sent his papers for conscription into the Tsarist army, and once a Jew was in the army he was never allowed to leave. Morris and his family trekked clandestinely to the Baltic coast, in terror that they would be discovered and sent back. Carl says: 'I once asked my mother how her father had managed to travel such a great distance without being detected, and she looked very furtive, and then she just said under her breath "Safe houses!" There was obviously a network helping Jewish families to get out of the Russian Empire, but it was very dodgy.'

Carl's maternal grandmother Anna Elenevitch was born in Lomza, a town in north-eastern Poland with a substantial Jewish population. Its magnificent synagogue was destroyed in the Second World War, and its Jewish population virtually wiped out. Anna emigrated to the USA in 1897, travelling by train to Hamburg and Antwerp, and then taking a steamer to New

York, where her family already had an established network of relatives. Carl says when he asked his grandmother why she came to America, she answered simply: 'Because there was nothing. We were starving.' At that time the USA was willing to accept an unlimited number of European refugees, but inevitably the policy changed. By the 1920s a quota system had been introduced, permitting the annual entry of only a tiny percentage of the various ethnic groups already present in the USA – a policy that later proved fatal for many European Jews fleeing the Nazis.

Carl's maternal grandparents met and married at some point after his grandfather's arrival in 1905. Sara, Carl's mother, was born on 25 April 1910, two months after her future husband. Carl's paternal grandfather, David Davis, had emigrated via Rotterdam to the USA in March 1902, at the age of twenty. David probably changed his name to Davis when he arrived at Ellis Island, where his naturalisation papers were prepared, and he already had family members, an uncle or a brother, living in Brooklyn under the surname of Davis. Carl Davis thinks that the family's original surname may have been Chotzkelewicz, and they may have come from Białystok, also in north-eastern Poland, which the immigration official wrote down in garbled form as 'Balquist'. David Davis arrived in the USA with six other members of his family – one of whom, mentioned on his naturalisation papers, was Rose. David Davis's wife was named Rose, so he may already have been married on arrival, although Carl Davis says his own mother insisted that her mother-in-law had been born in America. David and Rose's son Isadore, Carl's father, was born on 15 April 1910.

Isadore Davis and Sara Perlmutter married on 3 April 1934, and Carl was their only child. He was born four years after Franklin D. Roosevelt won the presidential election, at a time when the Great Depression had thrown millions of working-age Americans on the scrapheap. Roosevelt declared he wanted to help 'the forgotten man at the bottom of the economic pyramid', and promised 'a new deal for the American people'. His Works Progress Administration transformed the national infrastructure and created millions of jobs in construction, land conservation, manufacturing and the arts, with landmark programmes starting up in art, music, theatre and literature. During Davis's childhood, New York's Manhattan skyline was continually transformed, with new skyscrapers such as the huge Rockefeller Center complex rising up to join earlier Art Deco icons such as the Chrysler Building and the Empire State Building.

The Davis family had a piano at home, and Carl started to play at the age of seven. He and his mother played duets almost as soon as he could play anything. 'There was a harder part and an easier part, and so I started with the easier part, and then at a certain point swapped to the harder part.' A piano teacher was found – and nearly lost almost immediately, when the seven-year-old was taken to see the Disney film *Fantasia*. It made a deep impression. 'What captured my imagination was the abstract filmic realisation of Bach's *Toccata and Fugue* – it really explained the way the music worked. The Toccata was like an improvisation – you never knew what was coming next, which appealed to me – and I always loved counterpoint and fugue. I went back to my piano teacher and said, "I want to play this." He said it was too advanced for me, so I turned to my parents and said, "Fire him!"'

Carl says he wasn't terribly interested in playing the piano per se, but in what it could lead on to. As a young teenager, he decided he wanted to learn a different instrument, and found the opportunity by attending an educational institution known as a 'settlement house'. The Settlement House scheme, which grew out of the Reformist social movement in the late nineteenth and early twentieth centuries, was funded by wealthy philanthropic individuals who wanted to redistribute resources to the less privileged. They established institutions in poor urban areas in cities such as London, New York and Chicago, where rich and poor students were encouraged to live side by side in a mutually supportive, educational and creative environment. Music lessons were available, and Carl says they cost hardly anything – a dollar a lesson. 'I walked crosstown from my high school to the Third Street Settlement, and said I wanted to study oboe. They didn't have a place for oboe, but they had one for flute. I settled for flute. There were orchestras for various grades, and I started to play flute in the orchestra. I didn't pursue it very far, as I wasn't so fascinated by the flute as an instrument, but it was a useful tool – it was my first experience of playing in an orchestra, and the stimulus of playing together was formative. I had to learn to count bars, and to work with conductors and colleagues. When, a few years later, I started to compose, the fact that I had had this practical and emotional experience was invaluable. I knew, for instance, that it's very difficult to make oneself heard on the flute. In a large orchestra, that instrument is always at a disadvantage, unless you play very loud and very high. When you sit down to orchestrate something, that's the sort of practical thing you need to know.'

Although he didn't pursue the flute, he continued to improve as a pianist. At this point in time, he says, 'I was a bit in and out of piano teachers – I would get fed up, and then meet someone else who was exciting and stimulating and I would start again. My level rose, but I was inconsistent. I continued piano lessons, but I didn't have any theoretical lessons. I had many different piano teachers.' Around the time that he was twelve or thirteen, Carl was also painting a great deal, although without having formal art lessons, and for a while, he says, he couldn't decide between music and art, but music eventually won out. While he was having music lessons at the settlement house, he had the good fortune to fall in with a group of singers, who were much older than him. 'I was fourteen or so, and they were all in their twenties. They took me on because I was so eager to play piano for them, for the choral and vocal repertoire they were studying. At that time, I was hooked on chamber music and *Lieder*. I was playing all the time, and I got through a huge amount of repertoire, which advanced me enormously outside of school and home. I realised I had to be good at sight-reading, and I practised assiduously. I was precocious as hell.'

By this time he had also made a tentative foray into composition. 'I had done some composition as a child. As soon as I got to grips with notation, I announced that I was going to write an opera! What I decided I needed was the ability to sing and play the piano at the same time. I found a series of haikus in a collection of poetry, which were a good length – only seven syllables – so I thought I would play a piano introduction, turn to my audience and sing the words, and then play a postlude. I wrote quite a few of these, but then I destroyed them during a bout of negativism! Later on, because I was still torn between playing and composing, I had some formal composition lessons.'

After several years at a private high school, Carl went, aged seventeen, to Queens College, part of the City University of New York, for his first year of higher education. He says it was a stop-gap year, while he tried to work out what he wanted to do. 'I took part in opera workshops, did some Gilbert & Sullivan and so on, and during that year I formulated a plan of thinking that I could have a career in opera as an accompanist. I often used to go to performances at the Metropolitan Opera (standing room only, which accounts for my very bad feet later in life!) but before that I always listened to the Saturday afternoon opera broadcasts on the radio. I knew from the monthly listings what the classical music stations were going to play. I used to use the public libraries, which were very well stocked, and get the scores out, so I would prepare myself to listen to the radio broadcasts, following them with the scores. That was a very important part of my education. The broadcasts also included interval talks and opera quizzes hosted by a very interesting Russian-born educator, Boris Goldovsky. He combined a career as an opera director and conductor, and he had formed his own opera company based in Boston. He was a very ebullient personality, and I knew that he ran the opera departments at the Tanglewood summer school and at the New England Conservatory. I went to see Boris, and applied to go to the conservatory, specifically to take part in his opera classes. I could play well enough, and he recommended I went first to a workshop held at a place in West Virginia – an Appalachian setting, for about three weeks. Then from 1954 to 1955, I was in Boston, working in Goldovsky's classes.

'At the Conservatory in Boston I had to study piano properly, and work on my technique. And what was also interesting for me at that period was that the Conservatory was just across the street from Symphony Hall, the home of the Boston Symphony. The orchestra was conducted then by Charles Munch, who was also director of the Berkshire Music Festival and Tanglewood. As you can imagine, they did a lot of French music, and as a student, I had easy access to symphony concerts. The second hall, the recital hall, was in the Conservatory itself. I heard Fischer-Dieskau, Schwarzkopf, Irmgard Seefried, Dame Myra Hess, at their peak. I was exposed to a huge amount of music, it was very stimulating.'

While Davis was at the New England Conservatory, he was also mentored by Felix Wolfes, a German refugee who had studied with Reger, Richard Strauss and Hans Pfitzner, and had edited and prepared the vocal scores of several operas by both Strauss and Pfitzner, as well as working as an opera conductor. Wolfes had left Germany in 1933, moving first to Paris, where he assisted Stravinsky on the premiere of *Persephone*, and then to New York, where he worked as assistant conductor at the Met. He had been teaching at the New England Conservatory since 1948. Davis says that Wolfes, who was forty years older than him, taught him informally, working on opera scores, and became a great friend. 'He was a musician of an extraordinary level, and he also wrote beautiful post-Romantic *Lieder*, which sadly are totally neglected.'

In the spring of 1955, Davis experienced a breakthrough moment in his career. 'The Boston Symphony and the Conservatory Choir were preparing a recording for RCA Victor of Ravel's *Daphnis and Chloe*, and no one wanted to play for the rehearsals. They all opted out because the score was so hard. They asked me if I would like to do it, and I said: "Like a shot!" Charles Munch was conducting the recording, but they had this glossy idea of booking Robert Shaw, America's most prestigious choral conductor, to prepare the chorus for the recording.

'I played the rehearsals for Shaw, and *Daphnis* is a fistful of notes. But I did it. One of the knock-on results of that experience was that in my most recent ballet, about the life of Nijinsky, I was offered the chance to use a chorus in addition to the orchestra, and I went right back to how Ravel added a wordless chorus to the last act of *Daphnis and Chloe*. Ravel must have got the idea from Debussy's Third Nocturne, *Sirènes*, and I think the finale of *Daphnis* must have been inspired by the finale of Rimsky-Korsakov's *Scheherezade*, which plays a big part in my Nijinsky ballet. I picked up a fantastic amount of choral tricks from Shaw – how, when the chorus is singing wordlessly (*bouche fermé*) they're not just humming. Shaw applied syllables, he used a made-up language. I borrowed that shamelessly!

'Shaw had just lost his regular accompanist, and he needed one for his spring tour with the Robert Shaw Chorale. So he asked me. By that time, I was eighteen, and I said, "Yes, of course." I had to learn a lot of piano solos, and how to use an electric organ, which was an alien instrument for a pianist. That was my first legitimate step into the professional world.

'After that tour, I spent the summer of '55 in the opera department at Tanglewood, but then Shaw asked me to rejoin the Chorale for his autumn–winter tour. I left the Conservatory and did three tours altogether with the Chorale, and also had a summer season, in which we made several recordings – opera choruses, white spirituals and male glees. It was amazing to work with someone so incredibly gifted but he was wildly erratic, very emotional and difficult. I was a brat at the time, I was very difficult myself, but boy, did it teach me about how to work with someone who was incredibly professional. The keyboard player has to hold it all together; you must be in the conductor's pocket all the time. I also had to be responsible for myself – I had to succeed, there was no protection. We toured all over the USA, a bit of Canada, part of Mexico. It was the first time I'd been away from the East Coast – I saw the West, I saw the Mississippi, all from a bus. It was what I call my Whitman years, being exposed to American culture, after the enclosed world of New York. It was very stimulating, touring with an orchestra of around 20, and 32 singers. I learned that touring requires a lot of personal organisation. We did a huge amount of repertoire – the Mozart

Vespers and *Requiem*, the Bach *Magnificat* and *Jesu meine Freude*, Brahms's *Lieder* and *Liebeslieder* waltzes, some Schubert male-voice partsongs with piano accompaniment, Charles Ives pieces, and a complete performance of Honegger's *King David*. It was my first experience of working with a company.

'Many years later I had an interesting return to Robert Shaw. For decades he was the principal conductor of the Atlanta Symphony Orchestra. The orchestra had booked me to go over to do the Chaplin film *City Lights*. When I arrived at the hall, I found that I'd been allocated Shaw's own star dressing-room. Then I had a phone call from Florence Kopleff, a contralto in the Chorale who unofficially looked after Shaw, saying Bob wanted to see me. He was by then well into his seventies, and I did wonder if I really wanted to see him, half an hour before the show. But he was very sweet, very charming. I don't as a rule like to have other conductors watching me, but he was very complimentary. It was a nice closure. He died soon after.

'My breakthrough as a composer came while I was on tour with the Shaw Chorale. We used to play a lot of chamber music, informally, while we were touring, and when we got to a city I would go into a music shop and buy something like a piano trio, that we could play together on a day off. One day I was in a classical music shop in Philadelphia, and there on a table was some blank manuscript paper. I suddenly thought 'I want to fill that!' Those pages looked so inviting. I thought I would try to write something for my colleagues, as we were sitting on a bus for hours and hours, and I had become very friendly with the singers and the orchestra members – they were my buddies. I wrote a little trio for two clarinets and bassoon – to be played by three people who were my particular friends. They played it, and then they said, "Why don't you write some songs?" I particularly liked the poetry of e. e. cummings – I thought he had a rather naughty comic streak that really appealed to me. I wrote three songs on cummings's poems, and they were rather fun – proper songs, with shape. My friends suggested that we should try to record them, so that I would have something to show. We were on a six-week tour across the States, and one of my friends came from Nashville, Tennessee, where we were headed to perform in ten days' time. He knew a studio in Nashville, which he booked, and when we arrived we recorded the trio and the three songs with Jayne Somogyi, a soprano soloist from the choir. We made a disc – no edits – and then I looked around for a place to go, to learn more about composing, and to continue my musical education. But my work with the Robert Shaw Chorale was a real turning point – it marked both my entry into the concert world, and my beginnings as a composer.'

II

MUSIC FOR THE STAGE

Theatre has always been central to Carl Davis's life. 'From childhood onwards I had been a very avid play-reader. I love plays. We had a lot of literature in the house, so I was reading many plays. As soon as I got to grips with notation, I announced that I was going to write an opera!' When he was ten, he found a play called *The Women*, by Clare Booth Luce, a New Yorker. A comedy of manners about the smart set in New York, seen exclusively from a feminine view point, it had no male characters at all, but it had been a Broadway hit in 1936, and was later filmed. 'I started by trying to set a scene, but I didn't change the text at all. I managed to set a page and a half!'

Davis's next attempt at a theatre piece would be notably more successful. After he had done three seasonal tours with the Robert Shaw Chorale, and by now aged twenty, he felt that he needed to develop his compositional skills. 'I thought that I needed to go somewhere I could carry on writing music, somewhere I would be protected and I thought of a place where people could experiment. It was called Bard College.' This private liberal arts college in Dutchess County, New York, occupied a beautiful rural location overlooking the Hudson River and the Catskill Mountains. By the late 1950s, when Davis enrolled there, it had about 450 students. Bard had been an early adopter of progressive education, and several prominent European intellectual refugees were on the teaching staff, including the political theorist Hannah Arendt, the painter Stefan Hirsch, the philosopher Heinrich Blücher, and the violinist Emil Hauser, one of the founders of the Budapest String Quartet.

'They had a formidable composer teaching there, Paul Nordoff, who was a colleague and contemporary of Copland – they had gone to Juilliard together,' says Davis. 'Nordoff composed ballets for Martha Graham and Agnes de Mille, and was a prolific writer in many genres. He was a tough guy, and he'd already shown an interest in music therapy, he was on the verge of devoting himself to that rather than to composition.' (Nordoff later developed an influential system of music therapy, in conjunction with his English colleague Clive Robbins.) 'I took composition lessons with him, we did a lot of theory. He taught me to be a composer. I was with him for two years, and he challenged me. It was at Bard that I did my first dance pieces, my first song cycles, my first theatre music – and acted, and danced a bit, and studied the organ, while living the life of a twenty-year-old in a rather hippyish, but very beautiful environment in upstate New York. It all started there.'

Diversions

During the two years he spent at Bard, Davis met a young fellow student of his own age, a writer, poet and director named Steven Vinaver. Vinaver's background was similar to Davis's, except that where Davis was a third-generation immigrant, born and bred in New York City, Vinaver had been born in Berlin, the son of Polish Jewish parents. His father Chemjo was a composer and musicologist who had been chief conductor of the Berlin New Synagogue, and his mother, Mascha Kaléko, was a distinguished poet – her pre-war work had been praised by Thomas Mann and Hermann Hesse. The family had fled to New York in 1938 when Steven was still a baby – they got out of Nazi Germany just in time. Davis and Vinaver became very good friends. In their last years at Bard, as part of their Senior Project, performing arts students had to put on concerts, recitals, or shows. Davis and Vinaver, who was very politically minded, decided to collaborate on a revue, *Diversions*. Vinaver wrote the sketches and lyrics, and Davis supplied the music. Vinaver had been captivated by *Cranks*, a revue devised and written by the South African-born dancer and choreographer John Cranko, then with the Sadler's Wells Ballet. *Cranks* starred Anthony Newley and Annie Ross, and had transferred from London's West End to the Bijou Theatre on Broadway. It relied heavily on mime for its comic effect, an effect which Vinaver and Davis put to good use in *Diversions*. Their revue poked fun at many topics – urban living, Hollywood movies old and new, detective stories, and even the New York subway, in 'Subway Rag'. There were six performers, and 20 musical numbers – many cleverly subverting the genre itself. The opening number was titled simply 'Hello', while the customary ballad number was 'Here Comes the Ballad'. 'Musicians' was a nod to the music-makers. Act Two opened with a big production number called 'Production Number'. Scenery and props were minimal, and the cast simply changed their hats while singing Ravel's *Boléro* to nonsense syllables.

Diversions, described in reviews as an 'unpretentious musical with quality material', was a big success at Bard, and in the late autumn of 1958 it opened at the Downtown Theatre in New York, produced by Gus Schirmer Jnr, of the famous publishing house. It had a respectable run of 85 performances. 'Several influential people were in the audience,' says Davis, 'including Jerome Robbins, who was just about to do *West Side Story*. He spoke well of our show.' Davis's 'better than tuneful' music was singled out for praise. The show won an off-Broadway EMMY award, and its afterlife was one of the reasons for Davis leaving New York and settling in England.

Beyond Bard

Carl says he has been an Anglophile from birth. His parents' extensive library included a complete set of Dickens, as well as Shakespeare. 'I always had a strong inclination towards England. My light reading was P. G. Wodehouse. As a teenager, I learned a great deal about English music via the radio. I discovered English madrigals, Gilbert & Sullivan operettas (which were very popular in the US, where the D'Oyly Carte company toured regularly) and many other things. I used to listen to *Music for the Connoisseur*, a weekly radio programme presented by David Randolph, a choral conductor and musicologist. Its signature tune was the Vaughan Williams *Tallis Fantasia*. I remember hearing Walton's *Belshazzar's Feast* at Carnegie Hall, and also going to *Troilus and Cressida* at the New York City Opera. I knew Walton's *Façade* from an early age and I used to walk the streets of Brooklyn reciting it.' Years later, Davis says, he was able to repay his debt to Walton by rescuing his 'pulled' score from the film *Battle of Britain*, and programming a suite from it in D-Day and VE-Day concerts from 1985 onwards, as well as recording it with the LPO.

In the meantime, he had graduated from Bard College, and had to earn a living. 'Because of my experience playing for the Robert Shaw Chorale, I got a job with the Santa Fe Opera company and then with New York City Opera, as a repetiteur. The first season I was there, in 1959, they did 14 American operas. (Can *you* name 14 American operas?) The repertoire included the first revival of Kurt Weill's *Street Scene*, which I was later to conduct for English National Opera at the Coliseum in London. I also did a lot of back-stage stuff, including lighting cues and conducting the off-stage chorus. It was a wonderful experience. Singers were ringing me to ask if I'd play for them in recitals, and I was getting the reputation of being quite a prodigy.'

At the same time he felt that life with an opera company wasn't going to fulfil his ambitions. In 1958–9, 'it looked as if I was at the start of a promising career in the opera houses of New York and in the recital world, teaching and coaching. Then I thought, if I was spending twelve hours a day in the opera house, I wouldn't be able to compose as well. I know Dvořák played in the pit of the Czech National Opera for many years while he was making his way as a composer, and he found a way to combine both, but I didn't see how I could make it work. At that stage I didn't know which way to go – was it going to be pop, commercials,

Hollywood, Broadway musicals? I wanted to do all of it! Where did I fit in? I went to see a music publisher, and he told me: "Well, here are the choices. You can start at the very top level, and say you're going to write string quartets, a symphony. And then you could get a job teaching in a college. Then there's Hollywood" – which for a New Yorker at that time was the moon, but that was about film music, and that wasn't my idea at that time. "You could attempt to write Broadway musicals, but it's very rare to sustain a career that way. These are the choices you will need to make if you have to make a living." Davis wanted to be in the marketplace, but knew that he wouldn't have the time to do everything, and he wanted to focus on composition. 'So I thought, at the age of twenty-two, what I really want to do is to go to Europe. I'm a huge lover of European culture, but I wasn't sure where to go.

'I had a Danish doctor in New York – a lovely guy – and we had talked a lot about Denmark. I did some research on the state of music in Denmark. A composer called Svend S. Schultz, who was writing some great pieces and conducting the State Radio chorus there, was encouraging when I contacted him. With the support of my family, I thought, "I'll give it a go." I sometimes say that "I entered Europe through the back door", but in fact that's a horrible thing to say. What I really meant was that I wanted to wait a while before I attempted the big places. I thought if I go to Paris, Rome, Berlin, I won't know anyone, and I would have a language problem. This would be very daunting. Denmark, like all the smaller European countries, was very English-orientated. They speak English well, like the Dutch and Scandinavians.'

Europe

So off Davis went, aged just twenty-three. 'I felt I was being very brave. It was a long flight, by Iceland Air, which was cheap, to Copenhagen via Reykjavik and Gothenburg. The flight was delayed, so when I arrived in the middle of the night, the people meeting me had gone home. I stayed with Schultz for a few days, and he found me some excellent student accommodation, where I stayed for a term. Schultz suggested that I should undertake some general musical studies with Per Nørgård, who was only a few years older than me. He'd studied with Nadia Boulanger in Paris. At that time, he was writing what was, for me, incomprehensible music. Now I find his recent work much more accessible. But he was very patient with me, and very astute. I showed him my compositions and he gave me some useful tips.'

Schultz got Davis a job at the Royal Danish Ballet, playing piano for ballet classes. He played for the graduation students, the ones who were about to enter the company, and he was given a pass which got him into any performance. But after spending eight months in Denmark, he still didn't known exactly what he wanted to do, or where he wanted to be. 'I had no idea whether I really wanted to live in Paris, or Berlin, or London, and oddly enough, it was only by living in Copenhagen and travelling, that I realised that England had to be the place, partly for the English language, especially if I wanted to work in the theatre.

'By that time a new wave of English-language films and plays were finding their way all over the world – you could see *A Taste of Honey* in Denmark, and the film *Room at the Top*. English culture seemed so fresh – Tony Richardson's first films were coming over, and I had seen John Osborne's plays *Look Back in Anger* and *Epitaph for George Dillon* in New York, with their original British casts.'

But the decision was not yet made. Davis had remained in contact with Steven Vinaver, who had created a new revue at the Spoleto Festival in the summer of 1959, using some of Davis's music from *Diversions*. 'While Steven was in Spoleto, he'd met some of the people who were involved in Fellini's film *La dolce vita*. And he'd got some work on the production – the Italians didn't do any live sound at all, they built up the soundtrack in the studio, so language was no barrier – and he was working on that in Rome. He was receiving mail through American Express and I managed to get a message through to him. But by the time he got my message he was back in Berlin, where his parents had been spending a lot of time, and I went to visit him there. I went by ferry from Copenhagen to Hamburg, and then by train through East Germany. It was like a Second World War film. That was the only way you could get to Berlin.' Davis says that Berlin was amazing. 'The Wall hadn't gone up then, and the culture there was great. Steven and I travelled freely from East to West on the S-Bahn – Steven was involved in the Brecht theatre – and I saw several extraordinary productions at the Komische Oper, and Fischer-Dieskau in *Wozzeck*, as well as two productions at Brecht's Berliner Ensemble. Steven told me that he'd met someone from England who was very interested in *Diversions*.' That someone was Renée Godard, a former actress who now worked for Oscar Lewenstein, one of the founders of the English Stage Company and Woodfall Films. 'Renée had come to England from Germany in 1936 as a political refugee, and had done some films and theatre before she started working for Oscar. She was married to an actor in the Berliner Ensemble, and she commuted between London and Berlin. She was a friend of Steven's mother, which was how Steven met her. After meeting up with Steven in Berlin and talking through all the possibilities, these were the seeds of my move to England.

'But at that time, I still hadn't made the commitment. I was still thinking I might go back to the opera.' Davis had worked with some singers at Santa Fe and New York who were singing in Vienna in the summer of 1960. He decided to go and see them there, and check out Vienna, perhaps with a view to getting a job at the Staatsoper. He took the train from Copenhagen to Vienna. 'I spent five nights there, seeing *Der Rosenkavalier* the first night, and *The Marriage of Figaro* the next night. I had seen a production of that at the Met nine months earlier, with most of the same cast, but now they seemed very tired, and Karl Boehm conducted it so slowly! Then I located some singers whom I had known in New York. Lee Venora, from the New York City Opera, was at the Volksoper singing *Manon*, and we went out for a drink afterwards. She said, "Why do you want to come here? It's all dead here, all old hat. There's nothing new, just the old operas." And after I'd been to a performance of *Countess Maritza*, I realised that life in Vienna would be very limiting, and I was running out of money. I had a lightbulb moment. It had to be England. I love English literature, English theatre, English films; I relate to the culture.'

The move to England

At that point, Davis had just two English phone numbers. One was Renée Godard's, the other that of Steven Vinaver's agent, David Conyers. Armed with two possible contacts, Davis decided not to return to Copenhagen. Instead, he took the train from Vienna to London, a 36-hour journey via Harwich. It was the old *Kindertransport* route – the rail line along which around 10,000 Jewish children from Central Europe were spirited out of occupied Europe during World War II – which would feature in one of Davis's later concert works. He arrived at Liverpool Street Station on 5 June 1960. 'I asked the driver if he could take me to a hotel, and I ended up on Russell Square. I made contact with Renée Godard, and I spent a week going to all the theatres. I saw a show every night – the first one was Joan Littlewood's production of Brendan Behan's *The Hostage*, which had transferred to the West End from the Theatre Royal at Stratford East, and was in its final week. The ballet was wonderful: Frederick Ashton had just premiered *La fille mal gardée*, and I thought I'll see that, and I'll see the *Swan Lake* and *Sleeping Beauty* that I'd already seen in New York back in 1951.'

The twenty-four-year-old Davis couldn't have picked a more auspicious time to choose London as his base. Britain was on the cusp of the Swinging Sixties, enjoying an economic and cultural boom. 'Most British people have never had it so good,' declared Prime Minister Harold Macmillan in 1957. Unemployment was virtually non-existent and wages, exports and investments all rising. Wartime deprivation and the drab austerity of the post-war era were pushed to the back of people's minds, and Britain was looking to a brighter, more prosperous future.

The country was experiencing a building boom. London's war-flattened East End became a huge building site, as new high-rise tower blocks replaced insanitary Victorian slum terraces. It was clear that the car was going to reign supreme. Narrow streets designed for horse-drawn vehicles, together with inconveniently sited homes, fell before its inexorable demands for better and faster access. The M1, Britain's first full-length motorway linking London with the North of England, opened in 1959, heralding an unprecedented wave of road-building.

Britain's population, too, was shifting. While European refugees from the Holocaust were rebuilding shattered lives in the safety of north London, thankful to have survived, and keeping their mouths tightly shut about the trauma visited on them and their less fortunate relatives, new waves of immigrants poured in from the West Indies and the Indian sub-continent. Their reception was often far from friendly – landlords posted notices in the windows of rented flats – 'No dogs, no Irish, no blacks' – but with them came colourful African and Indian clothing along with the taste of exotic cuisine to enliven bland English palates.

Hemlines were going up. Mary Quant, a former art student at Goldsmiths College in south-east London, had recently opened her first shop in the King's Road – soon, along with Carnaby Street, to become a Mecca of youthful fashion. The short skirts of her stylish clothes, quickly copied on every high street, took their name from another British style icon, the newly available Mini car. Over the next decade, Britain would lead the world in music and fashion. While Elvis Presley was still king of the pop world in 1960, a young group of Liverpudlians calling themselves The Quarrymen were starting to play the clubs there and in Hamburg. Two years later, with a new name, and having been turned down by Decca Records with the disdainful comment 'Guitar groups are on the way out', the Beatles burst like a thunderclap on to the international scene.

Literature, art, theatre and music all reflected the new youth-centric, more egalitarian society, in which the everyday experiences of working-class heroes and heroines were at last finding a voice. The Angry Young Men – novelists and playwrights like John Braine, Alan Sillitoe, Arnold Wesker, John Osborne and Harold Pinter, as well as a new wave of young women writers including Nell Dunn, Shelagh Delaney, Lynn Reid Banks and Margaret Drabble – were tackling previously taboo subjects such as abortion, illegitimacy and domestic violence with gritty realism. The English Stage Company at the Royal Court, under its artistic director George Devine, was putting on Osborne's *Look Back in Anger* and *The Entertainer*, as well as plays by Samuel Beckett, Eugene Ionesco and Bertolt Brecht; while the legendary Joan Littlewood was at her height, with three or four productions running simultaneously in the West End and Stratford East. Her production of Shelagh Delaney's *A Taste of Honey* had transferred to the West End from Stratford East in 1959, and was currently running on Broadway. In 1963 Joan would stage perhaps her greatest production, *Oh, What A Lovely War!* Radio and television offered lots of drama opportunities for actors, playwrights, directors and musicians.

This was the scene into which Carl Davis – ambitious and hungry for work – arrived in June 1960. After a week in a hotel, he moved first into a small room in Southampton Row, and then, in the autumn, into a squalid flat in a Rachman slum in Notting Hill, exactly the sort of accommodation that features in Lynn Reid Banks's debut novel *The L-Shaped Room*. Steven Vinaver came over to join Davis in October, and Renée Godard got the pair a TV commission to do a musical, *His Polyvinyl Girl*, for ABC's Armchair Theatre. Then she engineered a meeting with George Harewood, the English earl who had just taken over as artistic director of the Edinburgh Festival, and was interested in staging *Diversions* at the Lyceum Theatre in Edinburgh during the 1961 festival. The show was a success, and transferred the following spring, under the title *Twists*, to the Arts Theatre, a small commercial theatre off Great Newport Street in London's West End. At that point Davis was taken on as a client by the legendary theatrical agent Peggy Ramsay. In 1960 Peggy was only just beginning to make a name – her first star client was Robert Bolt – but she ended up representing many of the most famous playwrights of the mid-twentieth century, including Joe Orton, Alan Ayckbourn and David Hare.

Carl Davis has always found live theatre a real turn-on in the broadest sense. He quotes Arthur Gregson: 'Theatre is a verb. It's something you do.' The real reason he had left New York, he says, was that he realised that if he carried on being a pianist, a teacher and a repetiteur for fourteen hours a day, he would never have time to compose. 'All my work in opera and choral music and so on did pay off, because I knew the inside of it, but I made the very big decision that I would become a composer, and attempt to live by composition, not performing. It wasn't just a coldly intellectual decision. It does of course depend on whether you have a liking for it and a gift for it.' His theatre work has always been slotted in between work for other media.

Steven Vinaver and Carl Davis contributed three musical numbers to a Michael Cochran revue at the Duke of York's Theatre, *One Over the Eight*, written by the young Peter Cook and starring Kenneth Williams and Sheila Hancock. For a while, it was a financial lifeline. Davis remembers: 'There was this wonderful time when I was getting two pounds ten shillings a week, and managing to live on it. As the show's attendances ran down, Michael reduced everyone's percentages, so that went down to one pound one shilling a week. I can remember feeling devastated, really shocked!'

His first West End commission, in 1963, was music for *Gentle Jack*, a rather obscure play by Robert Bolt, starring Kenneth Williams and Edith Evans. It was Bolt's first play since the huge critical and commercial success of *A Man for All Seasons* in 1960. 'I found *Gentle Jack* incomprehensible, and I didn't do a very good job,' says Davis. He found more success working for the (now defunct) Mermaid Theatre in Blackfriars, providing incidental music for three plays by Euripides, *Iphigenia*, *Electra* and *The Eumenides*, directed by Bernard Miles. He says: 'There was very little money for the musicians, so I dragged a solitary American trombonist who was working at the BBC Radiophonic Workshop into the production. Bernard said, rhetorically, "I'm looking for the Voice of God!" I got the trombonist, Nat Peck, to give a good blast on his instrument, and Bernard said, "Yes! That *was* the Voice of God!" In actual fact it was just one New Yorker!'

40 Years On

While the scores that Carl Davis composed for the Mermaid were the true starting point of his career in theatre, the breakthrough came in October 1968 when he was invited to work on Alan Bennett's *40 Years On* at the Apollo Theatre in Shaftesbury Avenue. 'It was Alan's first big hit. Up to then he was known for *Beyond the Fringe*, with Peter Cook, Dudley Moore and Jonathan Miller, and he had done some TV sketches. *40 Years On* was the first time he found a real voice in the theatre. It was set in a British public school called Albion House, where the pupils are putting on an end-of-term play for parents. John Gielgud played the headmaster, Paul Eddington the assistant head, and Alan Bennett himself played another of the teachers. I was musical director and arranger. Even though I had been in England for eight years by then, and was aged thirty-two, I found it difficult having to control twenty adolescents who were pretending to be students at a seedy public school. I wasn't even sure what a public school was, in the English sense. I was responsible for the boys' vocal performance, and that was very hard, because during a run, every night should ideally be the same. All you are trying to do is keep it the same, but it still has to be alive. Doing a run in the theatre was very interesting in terms of the discipline required.

'The lads were absolutely splendid. At one point they sang the Eton Boating Song, accompanied by guitar, and the guitarist later became a distinguished composer called George Fenton. There's a special way people sing the Eton Boating Song, and the way I did it disturbed Alan, who is extremely precise in his writing. At that time, it didn't occur to me that you needed to research these things – like the setting of the hymn "All people that on earth do dwell". Alan would say to me: "This doesn't sound right, it's not the way we sing it!" At least I got the Harrow School song "40 Years On" right.

'That show gave me a very valuable outlet. The director, Patrick Garland, went on to great glory before his untimely death. We did two TV films together, including *The Snow Goose*, and developed a terrifically strong relationship.'

40 Years On led to Davis being invited in 1973 to write music for another Alan Bennett play, *Habeas Corpus*. It was Bennett's third stage play, and starred Alec Guinness and Margaret Courtenay. Ronald Eyre directed. 'My idea for the score was to write it for a cinema organ – rather prophetic! – and there were several in London at that time which were still functioning, including one at a huge old Granada cinema at Clapham Junction, which has since been turned into flats. We recorded the whole score on this cinema organ, and that score began to have an independent life of its own, because people began to hire it to use in their own productions of the play.'

In between those two Bennett plays, Davis says he started working with the writer and actor John Wells on several projects. 'Without knowing John personally at the time, I knew his satiric gift and suggested him for these projects. One was an *Alice in Wonderland* for the Yvonne Arnaud Theatre in Guildford, but it proved too upmarket for what they wanted, and wasn't performed till much later. It finally achieved first a BBC production in 1973, and then a theatre premiere at the Lyric in Hammersmith. It was very successful, and was revived at the West Yorkshire Playhouse in 2005 and a year later at the Birmingham Rep. John and I also did an Aristophanes adaptation called *Peace* for the Mermaid Theatre. Again, that foundered at the time, but we later turned it into an opera for Scottish Opera, using schoolchildren as the Greek chorus, and contemporary popular idioms for the music. The third of my original collaborations with John stuck – it was a project for Joan Littlewood and the revived Theatre Workshop at Stratford East. John had a wonderful relationship with Joan Littlewood. They had had an outstanding success with *Mrs Wilson's Diary*, adapted from the *Private Eye* spoof series. John had a terrific gift for lyric writing, as well as being incredibly witty, and it was amazing to be working with Joan Littlewood – the woman who had produced *Oh, What A Lovely War!* She, too, believed that theatre was a verb.'

The Projector

'We worked on *The Projector* in 1970–71. For legal reasons, Joan and John had to pretend that they had discovered an unknown eighteenth-century play about the destruction of badly built houses in the East End of London, built by a corrupt Dutch speculator. In fact, our play was a thinly disguised satire on the Ronan Point disaster.' In May 1968, part of a block of high-rise flats in the East London borough of Newham collapsed after a minor gas explosion, just two months after the block had opened. Four people died and seventeen were hurt. There was a prolonged inquiry into the causes of the disaster, which found that structural inadequacies, design faults and the use of cheap building materials had contributed to the collapse.

'Joan had originally wanted to do a reading of the inquiry documents, but because of libel laws, they would have needed to read the complete testimony, rather than excerpts, which would have taken days. Instead she commissioned John and myself to write a kind of parody of *The Beggar's Opera* (a parody of a parody!), set in the East End during the eighteenth century. The projector of the title is a person who builds housing projects. John worked out the script to Joan's outline, and my role was to produce a score in mock eighteenth-century style. I claimed to have based my music on original sources, from a manuscript found in the Octagon Room of the University of Michigan. And it worked – the critics were fooled – even though the theatre was plastered with gigantic blow-ups of Ronan Point. We succeeded too well. Joan and John had created this amazing façade, and many of the critics were completely taken in. Philip Hope-Wallace, writing in the *Guardian*, even claimed to have detected traces of Handel and Bononcini in my score. *The Projector* ran for a while, but although there was talk of moving it to the Roundhouse, it eventually drifted away.

'By that time, I had already done *40 Years On*. Jonathan Miller, who's a great mate of Alan Bennett's, saw the play, and said: "Come along and do scores for my plays." So in 1970 I ended up writing music for Jonathan's production of *The Merchant of Venice* at the National Theatre, with Laurence Olivier and Joan Plowright. It was a typical Jonathan production, transposed to a parallel period, but all the women wearing correct corsets. I had the great thrill of working on that production with the designer Julia Trevelyan Oman. Her precision was an inspiration. I also did *The Tempest* at the Mermaid Theatre. At the same time I was asked to work with Toby Robertson at the Prospect Theatre Company, which was then at its height, touring productions with its new star Ian McKellen, who was having huge success as Marlowe's Edward II and Shakespeare's Richard II. I was asked to do the score for *Edward II*, and I also composed music for other Shakespeare productions at Prospect in the early 1970s, including *Love's Labour's Lost* and *Pericles*, as well as for Peter Shaffer's *The Royal Hunt of the Sun* and the musical *Pilgrim* (1974–5), with book and lyrics by Jane McCulloch based on Bunyan's *Pilgrim's Progress*. I also worked on a full operatic treatment of *The Beggar's Opera* for Phoenix Opera in 1971–2, which Toby Robertson directed.

'In 1971, Ronald Eyre asked if I would work on *Much Ado About Nothing* for the Royal Shakespeare Company at Stratford-upon-Avon. The RSC was also putting on modern plays at the Aldwych Theatre, and I was asked to write for some of its productions there, starting with *The Island of the Mighty* by John Arden, an ambitious play which was the source of a bitter conflict between its director, David Jones, and its author. At that time I was a mainstay of all the major theatre companies in London: the RSC, the National Theatre, the Mermaid and Prospect, which moved to the Old Vic in 1977, but didn't survive for very long after Toby Robertson was ousted in 1980. The range of plays I was working on was terrific. I did three more productions for Jonathan Miller at the National, including *Danton's Death* and the Beaumarchais play *The Marriage of Figaro*, with translations by John Wells. It was all going very well. I was working flat out, as I was also getting radio and TV commissions. I was certainly learning about multi-tasking.'

Marriage and work for children's theatre

It was through working with Joan Littlewood that Carl Davis met the actress Jean Boht, who became his wife. Born in Cheshire, Jean trained at the Liverpool Playhouse, and came to London in 1964 to work at the Royal Court and National Theatres. She also joined Joan Littlewood's Theatre Workshop company, but by the late sixties, Littlewood was struggling to recreate her earlier success, particularly after the triumph of *Oh, What a Lovely War!* which had transferred first to the West End and then to Broadway. She wasted a great deal of time and money trying to recreate a childhood dream – a twentieth-century version of the eighteenth-century Vauxhall Pleasure Gardens, with a theatre, shops and restaurants under one roof in a riverside setting – an over-ambitious project that never got off the ground. At the same time, Stratford East was being redeveloped. The whole area was a massive building site, a scene of devastation. Then in 1974 Joan's partner Gerry Raffles died, a personal blow from which she never recovered. 'We just caught the Theatre Workshop at the end of its glory days', says Carl Davis. 'Jean did three productions with it, and then suddenly it was gone.'

Jean Boht turned to television, where she carved out a very successful career, appearing in shows such as *Softly, Softly, Some Mothers Do 'Ave 'Em* and *Grange Hill* in the 1970s, and *Juliet Bravo* and *Scully* in the 1980s. Her greatest success was as the Liverpudlian matriarch Nellie Boswell in Carla Lane's sitcom *Bread*, which ran from 1986 to 1991. She and Carl married on 28 December 1971. Their first daughter Hannah was born in 1972, followed two years later by Jessie.

The arrival of two daughters gave an unexpected twist to Davis's career as a theatre composer. 'In 1981 Jean and I moved from a big rambling house in Streatham to a big rambling house in Barnes. The kids were seven and nine. Pamela Howard, a designer, director and friend who lived in Roehampton, advised us that the best school for our girls was Roehampton Church of England Primary. But we weren't living in the catchment area. Pamela had a word, and we went to meet the headmaster. I said: "I know that when the kids at your school reach eleven, they all do a show. If you take the girls, I'll write them a show." The Headmaster said: "Okay, it's a deal." But then, a year or so later, my bluff was called, and I had to provide a show. So they found me a writer, who had two boys at the school – she was Hiawyn Oram, a South African poet and successful author of children's books. Writing a musical was a new venture for her. We started a wonderful collaboration: the first, written when Hannah was eleven, was an adaptation of Hans Christian Andersen's *The Little Mermaid*. It caused a sensation, we had National Theatre designers, West End people, who also had children at the school. Mavis Gotto, a wonderful, inspirational teacher, produced it. She was very special, we would do anything for her. At this point in my life, I was beginning to take silent films around the world, but there I was writing songs for this show, sending them back from Tel Aviv, from Japan, and so on. There were deadlines to keep. The kids needed their songs! Hannah played one of the Mermaid's sisters.

'Two years later, in 1985, Jessie turned eleven, and she also had to have a show. We discovered that it coincided with the anniversary of the school having been evacuated during the war. This was a very emotive subject. Later on, it led to my writing the score for the film *Goodnight Mister Tom*, which was very significant. But this was my first contact with a story that had been buried for a very long time. People started to tell us about their own and their parents' experiences during the war. The story of the evacuation was contained in a diary that was still kept in the school, so we could look at it. We came up with a wonderful show, called *Vackees*. Jessie was cast in the role of a sort of Ginger Rogers creature who in Act II sang *Glamour*, a parody of a Cole Porter song.

'Those children's shows keep being performed – they have had an afterlife, and I still work with Hiawyn Oram, principally on concert works. There was another spin-off – the father of the girl who played the first Mermaid was the actor and playwright David Goodison. A year later he rang up and said he was working with the producer David Conville on an adaptation of Kenneth Grahame's *The Wind in the Willows*, which was coming out of copyright and he asked if I would do a score. It opened in Leicester and later had a spectacular run at the Chichester Festival Theatre. It proved very popular and was last produced at the open-air theatre in Regent's Park.'

The Liverpool-born theatre producer Bill Kenwright says that while Davis's theatrical work is maybe not as well known as his film and television catalogue, it epitomises the passion embedded in his notes. 'The one thing I always get when I speak to Carl is his enthusiasm for his musical adaptations like *Alice in Wonderland* and *The Little Mermaid*. He seems to still have all of the hunger, enthusiasm and boyish joy he obviously had when he was a successful off-Broadway composer in the early sixties. I love that enthusiasm.'

III

MUSIC FOR TV AND RADIO

From the moment he embarked on his career as a composer after settling in London, Carl Davis has shown himself to be fluent in many different genres. Some of the most enticing opportunities for a versatile young composer willing to work to a brief lay in the fields of television and radio. By 1960 three-quarters of British households owned a television set, and the medium was growing ever more insatiable for content, even though at that point there were only two channels – BBC and ITV. BBC2 arrived in 1964, and by the end of the decade all three channels were broadcasting in colour.

Early works for television

Davis's first television commission was for ABC's Armchair Theatre in 1961, the same year as his revue *Diversions*, written in collaboration with his American friend and colleague Steven Vinaver, reached the Edinburgh Festival. 'Armchair Theatre was leading the way with new writers,' says Davis, 'and its Canadian producer Sydney Newman commissioned a musical that Steven and I wrote called *His Polyvinyl Girl*. It starred John Fortune (later a mainstay of theatrical and media satire), and Nyree Dawn Porter (an up-and-coming young actress who later made her name in the hugely successful BBC adaptation of *The Forsyte Saga*). It was completely mad, no one had any experience of this. The production techniques were still quite primitive, and editing tape spoilt it for re-use, so we did it quasi-live. Charles Mackerras conducted it!'

There were no further television commissions for a while, but after *Diversions* (renamed *Twists*) transferred to the Arts Theatre in March 1962, Davis was taken on as a client by Peggy Ramsay. 'Peggy had a contact at the BBC's arts and cultural radio network, the Third Programme, who was interested in commissioning me to compose the music for some radio drama. My first real patron there was the Dutch director H. B. Fortuin, who was producing drama in English – he was very clever, very intelligent, very ambitious. He instantly taught me how to organise the music for a radio play, and in 1963 I wrote the music for a radio drama called *The Flip Side*. It was a satire on a late-night American DJ show, and I had to do very short bits of pop songs, bits of commercials. It was quite complex, and I managed to involve the jazz singer Annie Ross. She performed all the songs brilliantly. It did well, and the programme won an Italia Prize. H. B. Fortuin had me do many more projects, including Brecht's *Fear and Misery of the Third Reich*, and then other directors started to take me up, including John Tydeman, with whom I did an *Edward II*, and later an *Antony and Cleopatra*. I was in business.'

Davis says that looking at the nuts and bolts of how radio drama is put together is very instructive. 'I had very good experiences. Then there began to be a cross-over into TV, and after BBC2 opened in 1964 one of the actor-producers, Cedric Messina, gave me my first televised play, a trilogy by Ken Taylor called *The Seekers*. It was directed by a Canadian, Alvin Rakoff, who many years later commissioned my score for Channel 4's adaptation of Anthony Powell's *A Dance to the Music of Time*.' The following year, Sydney Newman, who by then had moved to the BBC as Head of Drama, commissioned Davis to compose a television opera, for which Peggy Ramsay suggested he should team up with the Polish writer Leo Lehman. *The Arrangement,* produced by Cedric Messina, was broadcast on BBC2 on 30 May 1965, and was praised by the critic Alan Blyth in *Opera* magazine. Lehman and Davis went on to do a second television opera, which has, however, remained unperformed.

The success of *Diversions* encouraged Davis and Vinaver to ride the new boom in satire. They had arrived in the UK at precisely the right time. The first wave of British satire, a genre largely created by a group of clever Oxbridge graduates, is generally agreed to date from August 1960, three months after Davis's arrival, with the opening night of *Beyond the Fringe,* the legendary comedy revue written and performed by Peter Cook, Dudley Moore, Jonathan Miller and Alan Bennett. Its success spawned the satirical TV programme *That Was The Week That Was* (known as *TW3*), devised by Ned Sherrin and presented by David Frost. A bevy of writers worked on *TW3*: some, such as Richard Ingrams, Bernard Levin and Peter Cook, were involved in the creation of the magazine *Private Eye*; others, such as Graham Chapman and John Cleese, went on to create *Monty Python's Flying Circus* for BBC TV. There were plenty of targets for their biting lampoons, ranging from politicians to the monarchy, sexual and social hypocrisy, the class system, and even the BBC itself.

The breakdown and reshuffle of established social hierarchies, customs and morals offered easy pickings at that time. Princess Margaret, the Queen's sister, had finally bowed to Establishment pressure to call off her intended marriage to Peter Townsend, the divorced man she loved, and in 1960 she married Anthony Armstrong-Jones, one of a new breed of society photographers working principally in fashion, design and theatre. Such an alliance would have been looked upon with great disfavour in Court circles a decade or so earlier, but within a few years the Royal Family was unable to avert a marital scandal when the Earl of Harewood, cousin to the Queen, divorced his wife and mother of his three children in order to marry his mistress, by whom he had already had another child. Meanwhile a naked romp in the swimming pool of a Buckinghamshire mansion involving John Profumo, the Secretary of State for War, and Christine Keeler, a nineteen-year-old would-be model whose concurrent lovers might allegedly have included a Russian spy, precipitated the downfall of Macmillan's Conservative government when the affair came to light in 1963. And in that same scandal-ridden year, the Duke of Argyll publicly hauled his duchess through the divorce courts, producing as evidence incriminating Polaroid photographs of his adulterous wife engaging in sex acts with an unidentified lover dubbed 'the Headless Man' (a subject that many years later would provide the young composer Thomas Adès with material for his first opera).

Steven Vinaver and Carl Davis were invited by Ned Sherrin to contribute songs to *That Was The Week That Was*, for which Steven also wrote sketches. The BBC pulled the plug on *TW3* in 1963 after only two series, ostensibly because political satire would be inappropriate in view of the coming General Election, but more probably because the BBC bosses were alarmed by the show's anarchic attitude. Sherrin went on to create two more satirical shows in the same vein, *Not So Much a Programme, More a Way of Life* (1964–5), also fronted by David Frost, and *BBC-3* (1965–6), presented by Robert Robinson. Davis and Vinaver worked as songwriters for both shows, but *BBC-3* proved to be their final collaboration. Steven returned to the USA to work as a lyricist on *The Mad Show*, a comic revue that opened off Broadway in January 1966 and had a successful run of over 800 performances. Tragically, that was his last project. In July 1968 Ned Sherrin broke the news to Davis of his friend's sudden death from pancreatitis at the age of just thirty-one, saying, 'I thought I ought to tell you before you see it in the papers.'

The producer of *BBC-3* was Jack Gold, who proved a central figure in Davis's subsequent media career. 'In the mid-sixties,' says Davis, 'Jack Gold asked if I would do a score for an *Omnibus* production of three short stories by A. E. Coppard, a contemporary of D. H. Lawrence. This was the first of some thirty or so projects I did for Jack, for television, theatre and film. He was so good to work with – a great friend and ally. In 1980 we did a wonderful but rather controversial *Merchant of Venice* for the BBC Television Shakespeare series, with Warren Mitchell as Shylock. He reminded me so much of my grandfather. He played the character in a very Eastern European way.' Although Warren Mitchell's portrayal of Shylock aroused howls of protest and accusations of anti-semitism, Carl Davis's score for *The Merchant of Venice* won him his first BAFTA award for Best Original Television Music. Three years later Davis composed the score for a further Shakespeare adaptation directed by Jack Gold. *Macbeth* starred Nicol Williamson and Jane Lapotaire as the murderous couple.

The fruitful collaboration between Davis and Jack Gold also embraced their first feature film, *The Bofors Gun*. It went on to include further projects such as *The Naked Civil Servant* – a 1975 Thames Television film produced for ITV by Verity Lambert. John Hurt won a Best Actor BAFTA award for his portrayal of the outrageously camp Quentin Crisp. The music budget was limited, as Verity Lambert was very strict about money. 'I said that with seven players I could make up a little band that would sound right. Jack wasn't very happy with my original treatment of the scene where Crisp gets badly beaten up. He suggested using some timpani. I replied that I had a 1930s dance band – they never had timpani. But Jack said, "Well, there's one in the corridor!" It was wheeled on in a flash, and Jack got his timpani roll. The film won a Prix Italia.'

The Snow Goose

Apart from his collaboration with Gold, Davis has devised some of his most interesting and successful projects for television, starting in the late 1960s, when he provided music sequences for *Wednesday Plays* on BBC1, and the title music for *Play for Today*. He also began to compose for a number of short television documentaries, beginning with *The Lacemakers of Nottingham* for the young director Stephen Frears (in whose 2016 biopic *Florence Foster Jenkins* Davis makes a cameo appearance as a conductor). Then, in 1971, Davis got his first opportunity to write a sustained score for a feature film for TV. 'I'm a great novel reader, and part of the real fun of my profession has been related to novels. The first chance I had was for the BBC adaptation of Paul Gallico's wartime tear-jerker *The Snow Goose*, directed by Patrick Garland and starring Richard Harris and Jenny Agutter. Working on the adaptation of a novel, the novel itself becomes a kind of bible, the source that you look to for inspiration. The whole production has a richness derived from a book that works on many levels.'

Davis's score for *The Snow Goose*, which in 1972 was nominated for an EMMY award, was opulent by TV standards of the time, involving 36 musicians, and he later developed themes from it as an 18-minute Rhapsody for full orchestra. The principal themes include a slow, modal melody with the feel of a folk ballad, that represents the snow goose itself, an injured bird that is rescued by a young girl, Fritha, and which she nurses back to health with the help of a disabled local artist, Philip Rhayader, who lives in a lonely lighthouse on the Essex marshes. Over the years, the snow goose returns periodically to the lighthouse, as an unspoken bond develops between Philip and the maturing Fritha, expressed as a warm, major-key love theme. The story climaxes in the retreat from Dunkirk, from which Philip, who has sailed across the Channel to take part in the rescue operation, does not return. The snow goose – the symbol of his liberated spirit – is seen hovering over his abandoned boat.

As Davis was writing the score, he remembers a moment that occurred during the editing which exemplifies the kind of dilemma a film composer can face. Patrick Garland realised that the music that accompanies the child Fritha remained the same when she re-appears years later as a maturing young woman, but still wearing childish jeans. The Paramount producer pleaded with Carl: 'Could you put a dress on her?' He responded by re-clothing Fritha's music in warm string timbres. 'Carl!' said the delighted producer. 'You *have* put a dress on her!'

Another novel that inspired an extensive score from Davis was Aidan Higgins's *Langrishe, Go Down*, about the decline of a once wealthy Irish family in the late 1930s. It was filmed in 1978 as BBC TV's Play of the Week, with screenplay by Harold Pinter, directed by David Jones. The cast included Judi Dench, Annette Crosbie and Jeremy Irons, who later starred in *The French*

Lieutenant's Woman. Davis thinks that the director Karel Reisz saw *Langrishe, Go Down*, and that may have been the reason, three years later, that he was invited to compose the score for *The French Lieutenant's Woman.*

Our Mutual Friend

In the wake of *The Snow Goose*, which won a Golden Globe for Best TV Movie and an EMMY for Jenny Agutter as Best Supporting Actress, Davis worked on a Thames TV series of adaptations of Graham Greene short stories, *Shades of Greene*. 'Whilst working on the Greene series, I met a director who had a very major effect on my style and technique. His name was Peter Hammond. He directed a couple of episodes of the Greenes, and we felt at ease with each other. He was really fun, as well as tortured – the whole package. In 1976 he rang me to say he was directing a seven-part adaptation of Dickens's *Our Mutual Friend* for the BBC, in 50-minute episodes, and wanted me to compose the music. We realised straight away that we had a major problem: the series was scheduled to begin broadcasting before editing was complete. Episode 1 would be broadcast while we were still working on Episode 2. This meant that the usual procedure for producing a synchronised score couldn't happen because the scheduling had sabotaged it. So Peter said: "You must write a library for me, I'll show you how to do it. I'm going to give you some suggestive titles that I know will 'turn you on', and you'll just have to write me something and we'll make it fit." He provided me with a list of titles for *Our Mutual Friend*, and I had to come up with music that on the one hand might be suitable to accompany the decaying corpses that float on the Thames, and on the other, something Peter described as "Ripples in a young girl's womb"! That was my first introduction to a particular way of working – the library method.

'The music budget was strictly controlled, and we couldn't use more than six players, no matter what the subject was. These were the days before it was common to get co-production money;

there weren't these big co-productions with NBH in Boston, for example. But this restriction led me along an interesting path. Six players is a classical sextet, so if we think of it as a genuine piece of chamber music in its own right, something will be happening at any given moment. It won't be static; it won't be wallpaper music. It will be a score that really participates in the drama. I really took to this idea, and I wrote about 25 minutes of music for which Peter's "suggestive" titles got me into a particular frame of mind. It wasn't so much directly programmatic, but more about the underlying themes. Quick decisions had to be made, and if I had done my job well, we would find something appropriate for each of the various moods, and play around with it. It was really fabulous, the way it all came together.

'That was the start of an entire progression of work in which I convinced directors that this would be a very interesting *modus operandi*. It offered me the chance to write at greater length – a length that would produce a satisfactory piece of music in its own right, that could later be turned into a suite. I was genuinely turned on by this way of working.'

From the later 1970s onwards, scripts for TV adaptations of classic novels were arriving at Davis's door by the truckload. He used his 'library' method for several more BBC mini-series: *Lorna Doone* (1976), Hardy's *The Mayor of Casterbridge* (1978), adapted by Dennis Potter and starring Alan Bates; Peter Hammond's own five-part adaptation of *Wuthering Heights* (1978), regarded as extremely faithful to Emily Brontë's novel; Dickens's *The Old Curiosity Shop* (1979); and *Prince Regent*, with Peter Egan as the Prince of Wales and Nigel Davenport as George III (also 1979). More conventional techniques of planned synchronisation were adopted for other BBC mini-series, including a twelve-part adaptation of Dickens's episodic comedy *Pickwick Papers* (1985); *Treasure Island* (1977) starring Alfred Burke as Long John Silver; and *The Lady of the Camellias* (1976) with Kate Nelligan as Marguerite and Peter Firth as Armand. Davis later returned to that score when he was preparing a ballet on the same subject. 'I didn't re-use any of the music in the end, but it was useful having already worked on the same subject. Both the TV adaptation and the ballet were based on Dumas's original novel, not on Verdi's opera.'

At this period, Davis was also experimenting with new textures and instrumental combinations for his film and television work. In 1980 he provided the music for the seven-part BBC mini-series *Oppenheimer*, directed by Barry Davis, starring Sam Waterston as J. Robert Oppenheimer, the American theoretical physicist known as 'the father of the atomic bomb'. 'It was shot in the States, and I had this idea that the music needed to be very percussive. I used four pianos, and we recorded the score in the BBC studios in Glasgow. We had two grands and two uprights and percussion. The four pianos gave a very monochromatic sound.'

The Far Pavilions

Two projects of the early 1980s encouraged Davis to introduce new timbres to his scoring, as well as textures. Literature and films set in India were in vogue at that time. The 1983 Merchant–Ivory film *Heat and Dust,* with screenplay by Ruth Prawer Jhabvala based on her own novel, was followed a year later by David Lean's film of E. M. Forster's *A Passage to India*, and the hugely successful Granada TV series *The Jewel in the Crown*, based on Paul Scott's *Raj Quartet* novels. The trend dated back to 1980, when Carl Davis was invited to write the music for *Staying On*, a Granada TV film of a single-novel sequel to the *Raj Quartet*. 'This was a beautiful dramatisation, starring Celia Johnson and Trevor Howard (the original leads in *Brief Encounter*). It's about two elderly people who stayed on in India after the collapse of the British Raj. I wanted to use Indian instruments, so I sought a lot of advice about the principles behind Indian music and in particular how to use the sitar and the tablas, which the director wanted to feature.'

Then in 1984 Davis was invited to write the music for *The Far Pavilions*, a romantic TV mini-series for HBO, based on the epic novel by M. M. Kaye which tells the story of a British army officer during the Raj. It was directed by Peter Duffell, and starred Ben

Cross, Amy Irving, Omar Sharif and Christopher Lee. Davis says he reworked a very interesting technique from the music for *Staying On*. 'A lot of Indian music is improvised and modal – you have to determine the scales which the sitar is to use. The choice of modes is determined by the particular mood you want to evoke – morning, evening, love, sadness. Each has its own character.

'The music for *The Far Pavilions* was recorded at the old CTS studio in Wembley, opposite the old football stadium. I decided to combine both Eastern and Western players. I had my European instrumental group and my little Indian band, which consisted of a family – the father, who played the santur (a variant of the sitar), the son played tablas, and the wife played just three notes on a tambura. We brought in a carpet, and they sat on the floor (where they stayed to eat their dinner, which the wife brought in plastic containers), and opposite them was my string quartet, plus a flute and a cor anglais. Their music was all composed. We projected the film, so the Indian musicians could see the images. We had already had a discussion about modes. They just responded to the mood required at any given moment. It was lovely, it was like a free jazz improvisation session. The sounds were absolutely genuine. Then I said, "Could you possibly add a small Indian flute?" And they replied: "Well, we do have someone who could play, but he's not free on Thursdays, because it's stock-taking day." We found another day when he could leave the shop, and he was terrific. It was very moving.'

Silas Marner and *Hotel du Lac*

The Far Pavilions suffered from the unenviable problem of not only existing as a substantial three-part series of two-hour-long episodes for TV, but it had also been sold to New Zealand Air for in-flight screening. Carl Davis adds: 'Films are edited down for use on planes. We had to have two editing suites and two separate scores, which was an added burden.' Nevertheless, Davis's score was one of three he wrote in the 1980s which was nominated for a BAFTA Best Music for Television Award, the others being BBC adaptations of

George Eliot's *Silas Marner* in 1986, and of Anita Brookner's *Hotel du Lac* the following year. Both were directed by Giles Foster.

Silas Marner stars Ben Kingsley as the misanthropic Victorian weaver who is falsely accused of theft and ostracised by his Calvinist north-country community. He settles in the rural village of Raveloe in the Midlands, and finds redemption through his adoption of an abandoned child (played by Jenny Agutter as she grows up). Davis's theme music contrasts an eloquent cello solo with modal, folk-like passages, while percussive sound-effects convey the monotonous clatter of the weaver's loom.

With Christopher Hampton's 1987 adaptation of *Hotel du Lac*, on the other hand, Carl Davis felt that this subtle study of relationships between men and women is in a direct line of descent from Jane Austen – the conflict between heart and mind. Brookner said that she wrote 'sad novels' and Davis's delicate score, featuring solos for alto saxophone and guitar, illustrates the emotional tension between Edith Hope (played by Anna Massey), a novelist who has come to a Swiss lakeside hotel to recuperate from failed relationships, and the outwardly charming Mr Neville (Denholm Elliott), whose suit she ultimately rejects. This was the first time Carl Davis worked with the producer Sue Birtwistle, who bought the rights to the novel as soon as it was published. 'I offered it to the BBC,' remembers Birtwistle, 'and the Head of Drama said he wasn't interested. I replied: "I know your wife does your readings, so take it home and show it to her." A short time later he phoned me back, saying that the BBC would take it. Two days later it won the Booker Prize. That night, I was woken by a phone call from America. It was the Disney Corporation, saying that they had heard that I had the rights to *Hotel du Lac*, and could I offer it to them. I said I was taking it to the BBC. "Have you done the deal yet?" I said I hadn't, but that was my intention, and they wheedled: "You could be big at Disney!" Nevertheless I stuck with the BBC, and the film won a BAFTA. Carl did a fantastic score for that – the theme tune, played over a view of the lake, was absolutely wonderful. He was a vital part of its success. It's not an easy story to do, with very few likeable characters.'

Pride and Prejudice

In 1995, Carl Davis collaborated again with Sue Birtwistle on one of the BBC's greatest international successes – Andrew Davies's adaptation of Jane Austen's *Pride and Prejudice*. Davis says that *Pride and Prejudice*, which made international stars of its lead actors Colin Firth and Jennifer Ehle, and became one of his most successful television scores, had a strange genealogy from his point of view.

'I had just composed a ballet based on *A Christmas Carol* for Northern Ballet Theatre, and I was trying to think of a follow-up, in the sense of finding another story that the public would know. It occurred to me that I had never seen anything done on *Pride and Prejudice*. I went to a meeting to pitch the idea as the subject for a ballet – which didn't go too well – but at that meeting a television producer was present who asked me if I knew that Sue Birtwistle was planning a TV serialisation of the novel. My agent contacted Sue, and got an enthusiastic response, and in the mid-1990s we started working on *Pride and Prejudice*. It was a tremendous success – one of the pillars of that particular genre.'

Sue Birtwistle takes up the story. 'It took seven years to get *Pride and Prejudice* on screen. I originally took it to London Weekend Television, because the BBC said they weren't doing classic drama. At that period – the late 1980s – there was a terrible prejudice against dramatising "old books for girls". I was equally certain that Nick Elliott, the Head of Drama at LWT, wouldn't be interested if I mentioned Jane Austen, so I just told him that I had found simply the sexiest book ever written. "Are the rights free?" he asked. I said they were but I'd tell him the rest over lunch the next day. When we met, he asked what the book was but, instead of telling him the title, I told him the story: "There's a mother who has five daughters . . . three of them gorgeous . . . small country town . . . shortage of men . . . then two sexy men arrive and disrupt their lives . . ."

"But what's the book?" he begged. "*Pride and Prejudice!*" Nick nearly fell backwards over his chair, but recovered enough to say, "I'll commission it."

Andrew Davies prepared the first three scripts, which Nick said were the best he'd ever read – but then the chairman of the LWT board declared that the network was not going to do classic drama, and the project stalled. Eventually I wrested it back from Nick Elliott, and the BBC finally bought it.

'I had loved working with Carl, so when I found that he was interested, I asked him to come to the BBC to talk about doing *Pride and Prejudice*. At that time, the BBC drama department had moved out of Television Centre into a 1960s jerry-built annexe by the railway line. The day I'd asked Carl to meet me was in winter, it was freezing, and all the heating boilers had gone off. He arrived with his big coat on, and soon we were terribly cold. The only place I knew that might be warmer was the canteen. I said: "It's early, there won't be many people there. Let's go and talk there and have a coffee." In fact, the canteen was absolutely packed, because so many people had deserted their icy offices and moved to the canteen to work. Everybody was hunched over their computers, in complete silence. We found a table by the window. Carl said: "I've got a brilliant idea for the song that Mary should sing to embarrass them at the Netherfield ball." And in this packed, silent canteen, he threw back his head, one arm in the air, and in a raucous falsetto, sang the opening phrase of Handel's aria *Ombra mai fù*. Everyone stopped what they were doing and stared. Carl just burst out laughing. I thought: "This is irresistible!"

'Before we start on a project, we talk a great deal about what music is needed, and go through the scripts. I always like to work with a composer before we start on anything, not only because the programmes need a lot of music, but because I always like the composer to work ahead. The music and dancing for *Pride and Prejudice* were completely different for each scene and were discussed in great detail, long before filming started. I met with Simon Langton the director and Jane Gibson the choreographer at Carl's house, and went through everything we needed. Singing, playing the piano and dancing are all part of Austen's storyline, not just incidental. The musical interludes move the story forwards, and how they do or don't succeed is integral to the plot. We had some wonderful sessions. Jane and I worked out the steps for the dances, while Carl sat at the piano and played. It was so much fun.'

Davis says that he looked around for the sort of dance music that would have been played at the time, and what size of ensemble it would need. 'Traditional country dances from the seventeenth century onwards would have still been in the repertoire. These dances were published together with the steps, so the authentic choreography can be reconstructed. It certainly gave it the right look and feel for the period. For the two ball scenes we wanted a contrast. The dance in the Meryton Assembly Rooms needed a rough, quite crude sound – it was a very provincial affair, like a village hop, so we used a trio playing authentic instruments. The musicians we found were really village players who provided the music for barn dances. Their coarse, vigorous sound was just right. For the Netherfield ball (a much grander occasion) we imagined that the musicians would have been shipped in from London, so we used a larger, more sophisticated group of eighteen musicians.'

'The designer gave everyone appropriate settings,' says Sue Birtwistle. 'Lady Catherine de Bourgh, who is an older character, was given a Restoration house with formal gardens and Carl suggested that the music associated with her should move back in time, it should be something like Handel. The younger or less well-off characters would have more contemporary houses and needed appropriate music from the Regency period. The feeling has to be right for everybody. We worked out which sort of musical style would suit each character.' Davis agrees. 'I had to think carefully about the character of the sound. I wanted to convey the sense of a small town in 1813. The model I started from was the Beethoven septet, which dates from that period. It was enormously popular at the time, and I thought that was the sound I wanted for the intimate scenes in *Pride and Prejudice*.

'My first job was to select the music that the TV audience would see being played or danced or sung by the characters on screen. This "source music" has to be authentic, just as the locations and costumes were. All well-born young ladies then were expected to play and sing, and to show off these accomplishments at balls, parties and home entertainments. It was all part of the mating game. To get an idea of the kind of keyboard music Jane Austen herself would have heard and played, I consulted her own musical notebooks, which are available. She copied out music for her own use, a common practice in the early nineteenth century. I don't think she went in for much Beethoven! Maybe a little Handel and Mozart, but mostly the second- or third-rate piano composers of the day: Pleyel and Cramer, together with some Haydn. I didn't use a great deal from Jane's own notebooks, but I tried to think of myself as a not very talented student of Haydn or Mozart, and decided that the music should sound like that.

'The real fun was choosing music that adds to the dynamic of a scene. Poor old Mary, who is the plainest of the sisters, grinds away at practising the piano, but really isn't very good. She's expected to churn it out at small gatherings where people want to roll back the carpet and dance. But when she insists on playing and singing at Netherfield, it's a terrible embarrassment. For that, we chose a Handel song, beautiful if played well, but sufficiently beyond poor Mary's range for it to be appalling. And then, to underline Elizabeth's embarrassment, we chose a very showy piece for the much more accomplished Bingley sister to play. It's performed very much as a put-down – the London set versus the Bennets.'

'If an actor has to play or sing,' says Sue Birtwistle, 'we cross our fingers and hope that they can actually play the piano. Even if they don't play, they are given a music teacher to show them how to mime playing in a realistic way. Occasionally we might use a hand double for the keyboard shots, if the music is very flashy. Emilia Fox, who played Georgiana Darcy, can play the piano well – it was all within her range. Carl wanted to play the piano pieces himself, but when he started to play for Georgiana Darcy's scene, it didn't sound quite right. I spoke to him through the intercom: "Carl, you're really heavy-handed!" He was a bit taken aback, but he did stand in as pianist for some of the other characters. Jennifer Ehle, as Lizzy Bennet, didn't play well, but in the scene where she plays and sings, the camera focuses on her face and Darcy's rather than her hands. That's the turning point of the story, when they realise they are in love with each other. Carl said that we needed to have a wonderful song at that point. He reminded us that at that period, operatic arias by European composers such as Haydn and Mozart were being published in England in piano scores with English texts, and young ladies would learn to play them in drawing rooms. I remembered then that when I was fourteen and at school, there was a particular song that had introduced me to Mozart. A new music teacher brought it in, and taught it to us in English. I thought it was so enchanting that from then on I was captivated by music. Carl said: "OK, I'll play it, and you sing it." It was Cherubino's aria *Voi che sapete* from *The Marriage of Figaro*. "That's the one!" said Carl. After *Pride and Prejudice* came out we had thousands of letters from viewers, and when I saw Carl again, I asked him if he had received many letters as well. "I've had lots," he said, "and every single one mentions the Mozart: 'This is a brilliant song, well done.' I think many people believe that I've written it!'"

Davis's title music for *Pride and Prejudice* made a particular impact. 'The title theme sprang out of an analysis I had made of the themes of the book. What is it about? I came to the conclusion that fundamentally it's about a conflict between heart and mind, sense versus sensibility. I wanted two subjects in this opening piece that would represent these two states: the piano semiquaver pattern for the mind, and the lyric theme for the heart.' According to Sue Birtwistle, Davis has a real talent for latching on to what the story is trying to do. 'This novel is about energy. Elizabeth runs everywhere, she dashes, she strides over muddy fields – it's sexual energy. Carl said we had to pick this up straight away – the theme tune must be full of energy. What gets the story going? There's a houseful of girls, and then these blokes on horses arrive – they're going to throw the Bennet household into confusion. And that's what Carl did with the music, he created a tremendous sense of energy.'

'The other main theme of the book is that women then really did have to hunt for men, and men hunted for women,' says Carl

Davis. 'It was all quite aggressive! So along with the keyboard passagework, I used some hunting horn motifs.

'Early on, we decided to feature a fortepiano, which would have been the right instrument for the period. One doesn't readily identify the sound, it's rather a half-way house of an instrument. But we found the right instrument, and the right player in Melvyn Tan. He was marvellous. I have since performed the theme using an orthodox piano as well, and it works as well.' Sue Birtwistle recalls that at one point during the music recording, the piano-tuner, who was also turning Melvyn's pages, went out to get a sandwich and was late coming back for the afternoon session. 'Carl called up from the studio, demanding: "Sue! Come and turn the pages for Melvyn!" "No," I said, "I can't do it." Carl wouldn't be put off. "You can read music, and the session's started. Come quickly!" He made me come down to the studio. I was so scared and shaking so much, I thought I would knock the music off the piano. But Carl insisted: "You are going to do it!" Just as Melvyn was about to play the first notes, the tuner came back with his sandwich. I've never been so relieved! Now, if I see Melvyn, he falls about laughing, saying "Ah! My page-turner!"'

'Alan Yentob, the BBC's Director of Programmes, felt that *Pride and Prejudice* had changed the public perception of the BBC,' says Carl Davis. 'Suddenly it was a sensation, and it continues to be, it's endlessly repeated. It had huge international sales and it opened the door to a revival of dramatisations of period novels, which had rather fallen out of fashion in the 1990s.'

Cranford

Davis's next collaboration with Sue Birtwistle came when she produced *Cranford* in 2007. Like *Pride and Prejudice*, *Cranford* had a protracted gestation. Sue pitched the idea to Jane Tranter, who was then Head of Drama at the BBC. It didn't sound too promising. 'There isn't a woman under sixty in it – they go up to eighty – and they're the leads. There's a cast of forty-five, most will have to be leading actors. The story is about the small details in their small lives, and there will be no fast editing. It will take the time it takes.' To Jane Tranter's credit, she commissioned it. The *Cranford* scripts, written by Heidi Thomas (who later worked as screenwriter and co-producer on the BBC remake of *Upstairs, Downstairs* and the phenomenally successful *Call the Midwife*), were drawn from three Elizabeth Gaskell novellas put together, plus extracts from her diaries, letters and short stories. 'We wove it together to make the series,' says Sue Birtwistle. 'Carl was familiar with the original novel, which was wonderful. He loved it.'

Davis had come across it years earlier. '*Cranford* was a period novel, and not very well known now, but it had a certain following. I knew it quite well, as John Wells and I had written a musical based on it. The TV series had a very strong cast, with Judi Dench, Eileen Atkins, Michael Gambon and Imelda Staunton.'

A number of traditional ballads are sung during the episodes, and Davis's title-music for *Cranford*, in the style of a Victorian ballad, captures the mid-nineteenth-century atmosphere of this comedy of manners. It is set in a small, self-contained community whose secluded existence is threatened by the intrusion of the new-fangled railway. He enjoyed working again with Sue Birtwistle. 'Sue is totally creative in her approach. If there is a dance, she will dance, and she really can play all the hymns and dances. A lasting memory is watching her whirl around my small sitting-room in Chelsea in the arms of the choreographer, working out the waltz finale of *The Return to Cranford* (the 2009 sequel to the first series). One of the few entertainments available to the denizens of Cranford was dancing, and the score includes music for a grand ball held at the house of a local aristocrat, a polka for a parrot, and village dances for the annual Mayday celebrations.'

'Carl adores working with actors,' says Sue Birtwistle. 'In *Cranford*, there's a lot of singing and dancing, and he often came on set, which the actors love. I try to get everyone who is involved in the production together at some stage. The camera teams, post-production people, special effects team, the location manager – everyone is invited to see what is going on at any time. I tried to get Ben Smithard, the director of photography, to come and watch Carl working with the musicians in the studio, but he refused – I think he was too frightened! On the second series of *Cranford*, I insisted that he should come, and he was completely astounded to watch Carl conducting all these brilliant musicians, dancing on his toes, so full of energy. "Now I understand what he does," Ben said.

'Carl is unusual in that he doesn't use any technological equipment to compose: he writes his piano scores by hand on manuscript paper. When we go to listen to what he's written, he plays it and sings the instrumental parts, on and off, to give me an indication of what it might sound like – things like, "French horns, French horns here!" When we did *Cranford*, Simon Curtis, the director, said: "I can't do this, I can't hear it, it's scary."

'Carl is absolutely wonderful to work with – he's so full of passion and energy. He knows exactly how to score for films. When we have a rough cut, he sees it, and once it is locked, he comes in and we have spotting sessions. We all watch the cut with time-codes, and say when we think a music cue should start. Any one of us can suggest the best place, and then we have to agree how long the music extract should be, what it is to achieve and if it should cut out or fade out. The process takes a long time, working in three-hour sessions. Carl takes notes, and gets a time-coded DVD which he then composes his music to, on the piano. Then we go back and make any changes. Sometimes we ask: "Do we really need music there at all?" Carl is very good, he doesn't insist on having music if it doesn't work at a certain point. He is often the one who asks if we need that cue, or if it would work better without any music. Quite often it does. I found that very helpful to learn. We go through the same process with each episode. Then the completed orchestral score goes to the recording studio, which is so exciting.

'Carl has taught me so much, just by talking to him, listening and watching how he does it. It's good that he thinks I know more about music than I do – in fact, I do now know more than I did. He gives you the benefit of the doubt and he teaches you so much about what instruments can do, especially if you show an interest. It's an act of faith, and it generally works. I can recall just one occasion in the whole of our collaboration when it didn't work. We were recording *Cranford*. Once there's a full orchestra in the studio, it's very expensive. They work in three-hour sessions, which can't over-run, so the race is on, and Carl gets very tense. When I heard one particular piece – it was quite short – it didn't match what I imagined it should sound like. It was very important story-wise to get it right, so I had to tell him it didn't work. He was very cross and it was quite scary. So I said, "Okay, let's take a break now and discuss it over lunch." I told him that I felt the music had been anticipating something that wasn't quite there yet in the story. He calmed down, went away and rewrote it; and the orchestra – all brilliant musicians – was able to play it instantly. It worked perfectly and even Carl agreed that it was better.

'When Carl finishes a session, after three hours, he has to go and change his shirt. The effort involved is so great. At the end, he is completely spent, and if I happen to be travelling back with him, I know not to speak, but just to let him recover.'

Sue Birtwistle has relished her professional encounters with Carl Davis. 'For me it's been a marvellous experience of working in happy collaboration with someone who is so talented – like having the best music lessons! From Carl I've had the sort of musical education that is priceless.'

Goodnight Mister Tom and war films

Davis's long collaboration with the director Jack Gold (who died in 2015) ended when they worked together for the last time in 1998 on *Goodnight Mister Tom*, a single film for Carlton TV. Based on a novel by Michelle Magorian, it starred John Thaw as the grumpy and reclusive old man who takes in William (played by Nick Robinson), a ten-year-old boy evacuated from London during the Blitz. '*Goodnight Mister Tom* was Carlton's swansong, but incredibly successful; it had huge DVD sales. John Thaw gave a beautiful performance. In a sense it was quite a conventional film, it just told the story. It was complete in itself – it just needed film music. You do the moods: music for the arrival of the evacuees, music to accompany the scene where Tom takes Willie fishing and introduces him to the pleasures of the countryside; music for the return to London, where Tom searches for Willie in the blitzed East End, and finds him among the ruins holding his dead baby sister; and the optimistic finale when Tom adopts the orphaned Willie and the two look forward to a brighter future.

'The theme of an evacuated child was one that I had explored in *Vackees*, the musical I wrote in 1985 for my daughters' school. So my heart was in the right place. The two world wars are such a central theme in British people's lives, especially for those who lived through them. They were exciting, and disturbing, and deadly. Of course I was brought up on the other side of the Atlantic, but I read newspapers even as a very young child, and I was conscious of the progress of the war, though we didn't experience it directly. It entered my nightmares, which I still have, of being in trouble at some period during the war and of having to hide or flee or else be captured.'

Goodnight Mister Tom was the fourth war-related film on which Carl Davis had worked during the 1990s. The other three were TV documentaries, focusing particularly on the suffering experienced by European Jews during the Holocaust. Two of these, commissioned by the Simon Wiesenthal Center in Los Angeles, were directed by Arnold Schwartzman, a British-born filmmaker who moved to Hollywood in 1978 and three years later won an Academy Award for his Holocaust documentary *Genocide*. The first, *Echoes That Remain*, dates from 1991. Through a sequence of rare archival footage and live-action sequences shot at the sites of former Jewish communities, it builds up a poignant picture of a vanished way of life in the pre-war *shtetls* of Eastern Europe: the markets, the religious ceremonies, the holidays, and the ever-present fear of pogroms. Davis's score for *Echoes That Remain* draws on Jewish musical idioms, redolent with minor-key melancholy, to underline the tragedy of these once-vibrant communities and the terrible fate that overtook them. Schwartzman's subsequent documentary, *Liberation* (1994), dealt with the freeing of Europe from the Nazi yoke, with particular emphasis on the Holocaust. Davis, who had to compose his music before the film had been finally edited, fell back on his favourite method of creating a 'library' of mood pieces reflecting aspects of the subject, which he then was able to fashion into an orchestral suite of seven short movements.

Overlord, the opening movement, is a tripartite piece, positive in mood, but with a more reflective central section, suggesting the nervous anticipation of the troops waiting to take part in the D-Day landings. *Annihilation*, with its string-heavy sound and modal character, evokes Jewish suffering in occupied countries, while *German Aggression* is a pompous marching song, scored principally for brass and percussion, with an ostinato side-drum accompaniment. *Massacre of Children* underlines its tragic subject with a plaintive lullaby scored for strings. *Gathering Forces*, still war-like in its use of the side-drum, draws on a theme reminiscent of Holst's *Jupiter* (the bringer of jollity, rather than Mars, the bringer of war), to suggest that good will finally emerge from evil, as the Allied invasion forces mass on the other side of the Channel. As they advance across Europe, the horror of the *Death Camps* is revealed in a lament for hushed strings, with a plangent oboe melody. The finale, *Liberation*, is optimistic but not bombastic, beginning with a unison string theme with interjections on solo woodwind, and ending in the style of a chorale.

In 1995, Davis was asked to write the theme music for a TV documentary film about the Holocaust's most high-profile victim. *Anne Frank Remembered*, directed by Jon Blair and narrated by Kenneth Branagh, won an Academy Award at the 1996 Oscars for Best Documentary Feature. It includes interviews with Miep Gies, the Dutch woman who helped to shelter the Frank family, and with Werner Peter Pfeffer, the son of a Dutch Jewish dentist and his wife, who shared their cramped hiding place in the hidden annexe of a house on the Prinsengracht in Amsterdam. Peter and Anne's father Otto were the only survivors among the annexe's occupants. The film includes a few seconds of the only extant film footage of Anne herself, who appears fleetingly on a balcony, watching a pre-war wedding procession in the street below. Davis's music for *Anne Frank Remembered* has an independent life as a short three-movement orchestral concert suite. *Disappearance*, in which the insistent drum-beat of mounting anti-Semitism in Europe is contrasted with Anne's peaceful early childhood, quotes the *Kol nidrei*, and culminates in the family's concealment. The second movement, *Attic*, is devoted to Anne's theme – an elusive, dream-like melody featuring a solo violin which dissolves into a *Ländler*-like waltz. Her theme disintegrates in *The Death of Anne Frank*, but then reassembles and swells assertively, to underline the fact that the message of her short life can never be ignored.

The World at War

The theme of the Second World War had earlier provided Davis with one of the greatest opportunities of his life, introduced him to a key collaborator, and ultimately provided the catalyst for his creation of an entirely new genre. In 1969 a dynamic young television producer, Jeremy Isaacs, conceived the idea of making a huge documentary series on World War II for Thames TV. For the first time, the conflict would be examined from the human viewpoint of its participants and victims, rather than from a purely militaristic angle, and interviews with survivors of all nationalities would be intercut with film footage of the time. Narrated by Laurence Olivier, it covered not just the war in Europe but every aspect of the global conflict from the 'phony war' to the invasions of Norway, Czechoslovakia, Poland and the Soviet Union; the rise of the Japanese empire; Pearl Harbor; the campaigns in North Africa and Burma; the U-boat war in the Atlantic; life under occupation in Holland and France; the Holocaust and the implementation of Hitler's Final Solution; the war in the Pacific; the Allied landings on D-Day; the defeat of Germany, and the development of the atomic bomb. The series was over twenty-two hours long and was broadcast in twenty-six episodes from October 1973 to May 1974. It took four years to research, and the cost was astronomical: £900,000, which equates to over £13 million today. It was the most expensive British television series made to date.

'One day,' says Jeremy Isaacs, 'I was standing in Soho outside the British Film Institute. Jonathan Miller asked me what I was doing, and I said I was making a history of the Second World War, and did he have any idea whom I should ask to write the music for it? "Why don't you try Carl Davis?" suggested Jonathan. "Jack Gold says he's very good." So I met Carl, we talked about the concept for the series, and he agreed to write me a theme tune. Theme tunes in serial programmes or series are very important for fastening the listener's attention. In due course I went to his flat to hear what he had done, and he had come up with a quasi-military rhythm. I felt it wouldn't work. I explained that the series was going to involve a lot of vivid action, but also a great deal of misery, destruction and gloom. "What we want is a signature tune that embodies the emotions you might expect to feel looking at the suffering of the people depicted in these 26 episodes, together with the pride and positive emotion you might expect to feel learning about major military successes against the Nazis which meant that the Allies won the war and they didn't. So what we're looking for is both a quasi-heroic march moving towards a triumphant conclusion, coupled with the inability to put out of one's mind the misery that is war."'

'The thing about working in media,' says Carl Davis, 'is that the music has got to be effective right away. You tend to want something direct, not too subtle. You have to grab your audience. In a way, you must tell your audience what the film is about – is it funny, is there a red herring, is it a thriller, is it a love story? When and where is it set? You have to take all these things into consideration. For *The World at War*, Jeremy told me that the major battles of the Second World War would of course be covered, but the principal focus would be what it *felt* like to live through the conflict. What was it like to be on the ground in the Blitz? What was it like to be in a German bomber, or to be a Japanese kamikaze pilot? What was it like to live under occupation? What was it like to be a US soldier struggling up from the boot of Italy? What was it like to be liberated? He was treating it from a purely humanistic rather than statistical point of view. You can't avoid that, of course: war is about winning or losing, and you have to tell the story. How many tanks, how many casualties and so on. But it was the *feel* of it that essentially interested him.'

Jeremy Isaacs continues: 'We needed something that would precisely mirror the emotional tenor of the visual narrative, created by the magnificent graphics department at Thames TV. The series wasn't just three cheers for the British, the Yanks or even the Russians, it was about a war in which five major combatant nations, including Germany and Japan, played major roles, and it was also a war in which civilians suffered more in destruction and death than the men and women in the Forces.' Alan Afriat, the senior supervising editor of *World at War*, raised the suggestion that Davis might consult the music of Bohuslav Martinů, especially his *Memorial for Lidice*, written to commemorate an infamous Nazi massacre at a Czech village.

'Nowadays, with a feature film or a series, you usually start with a "temp track",' says Carl Davis. 'The film will already have a score of sorts, pieced together from all over the place, which will usually then be discarded. They are often very good scores, but made up of other people's film music. Or, even harder to dislodge, it might be a substantial piece of classical music. Sometimes the temp track is so good that you end up virtually losing the job because the temp track works better. Stanley Kubrick's *2001: A Space Odyssey* had a completely original score by a wonderful composer called Alex North, which is never heard because the temp track, with music by Richard Strauss, Johann Strauss the Younger, Ligeti, Khachaturian, and so on, was so fabulous. So North's score was discarded. Jeremy had his temp track for *The World at War* – Martinů's *Memorial for Lidice*. It was terrific, but a bit hard to grasp.'

'Martinů's music is dissimilar to Carl's,' says Isaacs, 'but he could see what we were getting at. He said, "Give me a week or ten days", and then I went back again to hear the results. This time I was immensely moved by what he'd done. I knew it would intercut perfectly with the faces on the screen – they were the key. Our brilliant researcher Isobel Hinshelwood had looked through hundreds of pictures to find distinctly different faces, each somehow helping to convey either the dignity of belief in what they were doing, or an awareness of the suffering that was consuming them. You couldn't really tell what nationalities they were except that the little child's face that appears and fades away as the music ends is clearly a suffering victim. When I first heard Carl conducting his beautiful, memorable music with sixty star musicians from the LSO, I knew it was exactly what I wanted. "What we need to bear in mind," I reminded him, "is that when this main title (which is the series' calling card) fades out, something else completely different might come clattering in – it could be troops advancing in battle, it could be women grieving over the dead. The end of the music must be ambivalent. It must be possible to follow it with either joy or sorrow." And he achieved that marvellously.'

'The title music was a big challenge,' says Davis. 'Because the programme was global, and had as much about war in the Pacific and the USA as about Europe, I thought that I needed to focus it somewhere. It occurred to me that there were certain harmonic progressions in Czech music that I liked, in Smetana, Martinů and Janáček, where you move abruptly from a minor key into a major one. That gives you a feeling of openness. I went into a "Think Czech" mode. And of course Czechoslovakia was at the centre of the European warring nations, and it's a small country which had always wanted to be independent and democratic. So I imbued my theme with a sense of striving. The theme also brings Shostakovich to mind. Three hours of the series dealt purely with the campaign in Russia, and because of my own background I was always very sympathetic to Russian composers, and to Shostakovich in particular.'

Davis's title music for *The World at War* – a portentous, string-heavy, chordal theme, with a questioning, feminine ending to its initial phrase – is one of his most arresting and memorable creations. Played over a haunting sequence of cross-fading faces, and then an image of flames obliterating the screen, it hammered home the message that this series was not only about war, but the pity of war.

'Carl went on to do the music for each of the twenty-six programmes,' says Jeremy Isaacs, 'except for one, *Genocide*, which had no music. The horrors we were seeing in that episode couldn't be adorned, lamented nor evoked any further. There was a deftness and delicacy of touch about the incidental music that he wrote separately for each episode. With the help of machinery he had installed in his home, he could run the images, and split second by split second, half a note by half a note, match what he wrote to the space available. I had a rule that in this series there would be three kinds of sounds: the talk of the interviewees, the noises and sound-effects of war, and music. That music could be divided into two chunks. Far and away the biggest chunk – around 95 per cent – was written by Carl. Sometimes it felt more appropriate to add local colour, with a French music-hall song and so on. The house rule, observed strictly by the dubbing editor, was that no one sound was ever to eliminate the other. They weren't intended to co-exist.'

'I wasn't being asked to produce continuous wallpaper music,' says Davis. 'The use of music in the series was very selective. There was a precedent with Wilfred Josephs' score for the BBC series *The Great War*, and I took that as my model. All the way through the production, we were always questioning. The style proved rather elusive to achieve until we got into it. The thing about contemporary film is that the soundtrack is made up of three components: dialogue, sound effects and music, and all your preparation, meetings and discussions end up coming together in the dub. That's where final judgements are made by the producer and director. They discuss how to make the sound track effective. Should it be purely dialogue without music, what sections should be done without music, when do we actually need music? At that point, we might realise that maybe parts of the film with no music sound-track might actually work better with music. Some film composers are very protective about their scores, but my own view is that music is continuously pliable. Does a particular moment

Top left Carl Davis as a baby with his parents, *c.* 1937
Top right Carl aged about four
Below Carl and his mother in Florida, *c.* 1980s

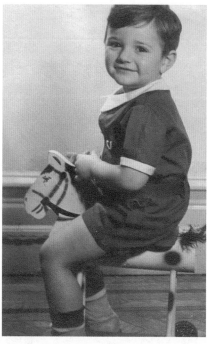

Above left The young Carl with
his parents
Above right Carl in 1938
Left Carl in 1946

Carl in the 1960s

Carl, Jean and their dog Charlie the basset hound
in a photo for a Christmas card

Left Jonathan Miller
Above Steven Vinaver

Carl in his studio at Streatham

Above Carl in the 1980s
Right Carl's 75th birthday party,
with Jack Gold

Working on a 2016 score

need the support, or the emotional underpinning, or the continuity that music can provide?

'Working on *The World at War* was the first time I'd been made aware of this continuous discussion process. Here are the tanks and machine guns and bombs – what would be the point of adding music as well? In conventional presentations of this material, there often is continuous music, but you can't really hear it, and you're probably not aware of it. Sometimes it might just be there in case there's a gap. The producers had access to soundtracks containing original music of the period – songs by Gracie Fields, Charles Trenet, Irving Berlin, Noël Coward and others – so in the main, when it came to what music I should write, it was my own music.'

'Carl's score not only gave great pleasure in the depiction of various episodes, it also played an absolutely vital role in holding the series together,' says Jeremy Isaacs. 'If the music had been wildly different from one episode to another, the whole series might have fallen apart. Certainly, its unity would have suffered. The great benefit of what Carl wrote was that he provided cues, like Wagnerian *Leitmotifs*, which turned up at appropriate moments to tell the viewer what was happening. For instance, if you saw tanks rolling and armies marching across what might be the Soviet Union, the music would tell you that it was the Wehrmacht. In the episodes about the war in Burma or the fall of Singapore, you could hear an Indonesian or Japanese influence in the music, even though the music itself wasn't indigenous.'

Davis is particularly proud of the short suite of movements he supplied to depict the fall of France in episode three. A lilting, Satie-like theme evokes the strange calm of the 'phony war', as French soldiers waited – apparently in vain – for the expected German invasion along the heavily fortified Maginot Line, while life in the capital goes on as usual. A melody on saxophone – an instrument closely identified with French civilian life – is disrupted by the insistent drum-beat of war as their army is mobilised, while the idiom becomes increasingly dissonant as the peace of the Ardennes forest is penetrated by enemy forces. The saxophone reappears later in the series to introduce a slow blues as US soldiers and airmen arrive in Britain, while the piano dominates the music which accompanies scenes of the disastrous Arnhem Airlift. Goose-stepping German soldiers are satirised in a pompous march with a theme reminiscent of Shostakovich's 'Leningrad' Symphony over a military drum-beat, while the devastation of Warsaw is summed up by an infinitely melancholic mazurka.

'Carl made a huge contribution to the success of *The World at War*,' says Jeremy Isaacs. 'The series meant a very great deal to him. He knew that it was a piece that people would remember him for.' Davis agrees. '*The World at War* was a highly significant project in my career. It has had the most extraordinary afterlife – it is constantly repeated on various TV channels and on other media as they have evolved. It is regarded as *the* definitive series about World War II.'

In 1998 Carl Davis was again invited to collaborate with Jeremy Isaacs on another huge, twenty-four episode, war-related TV series, produced by Martin Smith. In a series of interviews intercut with archive footage, linked by Kenneth Branagh's narration, *Cold War* examines the stand-off between the Soviet Bloc and the Western Powers which occupied most of the second half of the twentieth century. Davis's theme music for *Cold War* conveys a sense of scurrying urgency, as the camera pans along a bunker-like tunnel, past projected photos of Cold War world leaders, together with footage of deadly nuclear missiles. The theme expands as it travels forwards, but is constantly interrupted by sound crashing in from the sides. It ends with a question mark, as a solo violin plays a chord on open strings. The contemporary idiom makes it clear that we are living in a modern world, but one that might at any moment be threatened by annihilation.

Hollywood

In the wake of *The World at War* Jeremy Isaacs, by now promoted to Director of Programmes at Thames, rapidly initiated the next major documentary project in which Davis was involved. It was

1973 and it was to have profound and far-reaching consequences on his career.

'As work on *The World at War* was coming to an end and the series had begun to go to air, with ten programmes still unfinished,' says Isaacs, 'some of the people working on it were having nightmares about what they'd seen – the woman who had interviewed murderous former Nazis, for instance, couldn't sleep at night. I thought, "We've got to cheer ourselves up." We had a party, and I gave each member of the production team a paperback copy of a book by Kevin Brownlow called *The Parade's Gone By* – a title which I thought had an appropriate military resonance for our "World Warriors", as we called ourselves. In fact it had nothing to do with war, it's a marvellous book containing about 500 interviews with people who had worked in Hollywood in the silent movie era. I said to the team: "This is going to be the subject of our next series."'

Isaacs arranged a meeting with Kevin Brownlow. Films and film-making were Brownlow's passion. As a schoolboy at an austere boarding school in the post-war period, he was enthralled by the headmaster's weekly showings of old black-and-white movies on a 9.5mm projector, and had pestered his parents until they bought him a similar machine for use at home. In 1956, aged eighteen, he began work with Andrew Mollo, an expert on military uniforms, on *It Happened Here,* a black-and-white film of his own, and persevered with it for eight years until its release in 1964. Made on a shoestring budget and largely using amateur actors, the film dealt with what might have happened in Britain if the Germans had won the war. Eleven years later, Brownlow and Mollo followed it with a second film, *Winstanley,* set in the aftermath of the English Civil War. But this unassuming Englishman's sixty-year dedication to silent movies, during which he has travelled the globe tracking down lost masterpieces, has led him to be dubbed 'the Indiana Jones of the cinema world'. In 2010, this 'giant among film historians and preservationists', as he was described in Martin Scorsese's nomination, was rewarded with an Academy Lifetime Achievement Award – although he took the opportunity in his acceptance speech to excoriate the Hollywood film industry for having carelessly mislaid or destroyed almost three-quarters of the entire output of the silent film era.

'Kevin Brownlow was a film-maker with a nose for how to make a film,' says Jeremy Isaacs. 'He disdained television, and didn't even own a TV set until some point during *The World at War* transmissions, which he was kind enough to say were terrific films of great historical significance. I told him I wanted him to make a history of Hollywood for me at Thames in no less than thirteen episodes, making use of the marvellous interviews he had done, and that I would pay him to re-interview people for TV.

'One of the biggest decisions of my life was to commission those interviews from Kevin before we had gained the rights from Hollywood studios to use clips from the films. That was a long and torturous process. But it was vital to get these interviews, as the people Kevin wanted to talk to were dying off. Kevin couldn't believe his ears. He had been banging on doors for years, but nobody had ever asked him to do anything on this scale.'

'Jeremy warned me then that television was a very ulcer-producing activity,' says Brownlow. 'I walked out of the building after our meeting and promptly collapsed on the pavement in appalling pain. I remember thinking "This is ridiculous, I haven't even said yes yet!" It turned out to be appendicitis.'

Once recovered, Brownlow and his colleague David Gill, a former ballet dancer turned TV producer, editor and film historian, left for the USA to talk to the rapidly reducing number of people involved in the silent film industry who were still alive. Many of them had been working in the 1920s, so this was indeed a 'just in time' exercise. They returned with an extraordinary series of interviews, not just with actors such as Hollywood's glamour girl Gloria Swanson, but with producers, directors, cameramen, special effects people, stuntmen, make-up artists and musicians. 'Kevin and David were a superb creative partnership,' says Isaacs. 'Their approach to the series was wonderful – it was about how the films were made. It was eye-opening and hugely entertaining.'

By the late 1970s, Isaacs himself was no longer employed directly by Thames TV, but the management allowed him to continue to work on the series as an executive producer. In thirteen 50-minute episodes, *Hollywood* planned to embrace the entire gamut of silent film-making, from the early pre-First World War pioneers, to the end of an era when soundtracks came in. The series covered the introduction of the infamous Production Code to uphold moral standards; early war films such as King Vidor's *The Big Parade*, and Lewis Milestone's *All Quiet on the Western Front*, released in both silent and sound versions, which controversially depicted trench warfare from the German viewpoint; slapstick comedy and the role of stuntmen; the great romantic leads (Gloria Swanson, Rudolph Valentino and Greta Garbo); swashbuckling heroes such as Douglas Fairbanks; autocratic directors such as Cecil B. DeMille and Erich von Stroheim; the silent film comedians – Harold Lloyd, Buster Keaton, Harry Langdon and Charlie Chaplin; the craze for Westerns; the role of the director and the cameraman. The final episodes dealt with the coming of sound, and the ultimate disintegration of the silent film industry, as well as the disappearance from the screen of those stars who failed to adapt to the new sound-based technology. Only the American film industry was covered – a follow-up series on European silent film would be made a few years later. As well as the interviews garnered by Brownlow and Gill, the thirteen episodes, narrated by James Mason, incorporated over 300 clips from around 160 silent films made in the USA between 1894 and 1933, sourced from the very best available material, and shown at their original running speed, accompanied by orchestral scores provided by Carl Davis.

Hollywood occupied Davis on and off between 1976 and 1980, when the series was finally broadcast between January and April. 'I went to Washington and Los Angeles and New York to go to the libraries that had scores and memorabilia; but in Los Angeles I met musicians who had worked in the silent film industry who were still there, still playing. Our researcher discovered Ann Leaf, who had been the last cinema organist at the Paramount Theatre, New York. I asked Ann: "How do you construct a whole score for a silent film?" She replied: "You need a cupboard-full of material.

It's all about moods: this is good for love scenes, this is good for a chase, this is good for a battle scene, you need to know national anthems, popular songs and so on. Nothing is sacred, it can all be used." Ann told me that her husband used to sit beside her while she played, with a stopwatch, and they would time how long each section of film was. They had a system – he would warn her when it was time to change the piece of music.

'Ann said that, in general, the music for silent movies was mostly very conservative in style. The cinema-going public knew what they liked – sentimental ballads, waltzes, things that were pleasing or dramatically effective. In the 1970s in Hollywood there were still shops where this music could be found. The silent cinema era was a heyday for music publishers, as all the cinemas were demanding music. If you went to a big cinema in London's West End, you would expect to see the film accompanied by an orchestra. It must have been quite an industry, supplying musicians, librarians, arrangers. Some of this orchestral music still exists – I was able to find some, in second-hand bookshops. You could not only buy the score, you could also buy the orchestral parts. If a live orchestra was used in the larger cinemas, they might be playing for four long performances a day, so there were breaks in the middle where the orchestra would go out, and the cinema organ would take over for a while, but then the orchestra would return for the big climax. Most of the major towns and cities could provide an orchestra to accompany silent film showings, and in the USA, some films, such as D. W. Griffith's *Intolerance* and *The Birth of a Nation*, even toured with their own orchestra.

'There was always some kind of live element to film screenings. There are photographs from the early 1900s showing, for instance, how a shop had been converted into a cinema, and they were advertising how big their "orchestra" was – even if it was just six players! But in the end cinema organs supplanted orchestras as it was far cheaper to pay for one musician rather than an orchestra. The further you were away from the centre of town, the more likely it was that there would just be an organ. The big cinema organs – like the Mighty Wurlitzer – were specially invented.

They had sound effects – gunshots, and so on. I remember when I was growing up in New York, there were a few picture houses still showing silent films, and in the 1940s they did Saturday morning screenings with a piano accompanying them. There were also screenings at the Museum of Modern Art – and these still continue today.

'The range of material is enormous, because people made films about everything you can think of. There were no hard and fast rules, but you must always make sure that the music has something to do with the film. And nothing is harder than watching a silent film in silence. That is really, really tough. But I've done it, and it's good, because in my mind, I'm already preparing the ground for a score. I'm already composing it while I'm watching it.'

For the *Hollywood* series, Davis created a superb title-theme, a swirling, Viennese-sounding waltz in the old-fashioned romantic style. It conjures up an electric atmosphere of anticipation, as if a cinema audience were eagerly awaiting the lights going down and the screen unfurling. 'Carl told me that he wrote the theme tune in five minutes, in the back of a taxi,' says Kevin Brownlow. Davis's work on the various genres of silent films – though only excerpts at this stage – provided him with endless opportunities to tackle different compositional styles which he later expanded into full-scale film scores. A sultry tango complete with swooning violins, solo cornet and accordion, danced by Rudolph Valentino in *The Four Horsemen of the Apocalypse*; a voluptuous-sounding, full-blown romantic love theme for Greta Garbo in *Flesh and the Devil*; a lushly orchestrated score in the style of Richard Strauss, tinged with exotic harmonies and orchestral effects, to depict the decadence of ancient Babylon in D. W. Griffith's *Intolerance*; cheeky twenties-style jazz numbers for Harold Lloyd in *Safety Last* and for Clara Bow in *It*; the quintessential galloping rhythm of wagons rolling for Westerns; seductive Orientalism as Douglas Fairbanks rides on a magic carpet in *The Thief of Bagdad*; and the thrilling, Wagnerian-sounding sequence, punctuated by brass fanfares, and suggestive of the pounding of hooves, that accompanies the famous chariot race in *Ben-Hur*. 'The most exciting moment on *Hollywood* I can remember was when we had to make a preview to sell the idea to American TV,' says Kevin Brownlow. 'The moment Carl raised his baton and the orchestra began, it was so thrilling, even though it was at that time just a studio recording. You can just imagine the experience multiplied in the cinema.'

Davis's musical contribution to the *Hollywood* series has formed the basis for a huge body of work that has occupied him for the past thirty-five years. '*Hollywood* was important from a business point of view because the visual side was not reliant on dialogue. It relied on interviews which could be dubbed into any number of different languages. It was ideal for export. Thames found they had a real hit in terms of international distribution, particularly for the Continent. It was very accessible, and it went ballistic in its first year.' An early review of *Hollywood* in *Variety* magazine pinpointed Davis's role in that success: 'Carl Davis's music is doubly successful in that it's partially from original scores, partially original for the series. It helps the silents speak out.'

'When Jeremy Isaacs conceived the idea of *Hollywood*, he had expected us to use the same narrator and the same composer as for *The World at War*,' says Kevin Brownlow. 'In fact, the narrator had to be changed, but the composer was an absolute triumph. There couldn't have been anyone better than Carl. Not only did he go to America and meet the surviving musicians from the silent era, but he comes from that background. His knowledge of the world of the motion picture of that period, and its music – both popular and classical – is so instinctive that I always imagine he must go back that far himself. He must be aged at least 120! Yes, he does borrow from other composers – he jokes that his favourite composer is "Borodin" – but his taste for selecting the right music is almost uncanny.'

When *Hollywood* opened on Thames TV in early February 1980, Carl Davis and David Gill conceived the idea of celebrating the occasion by putting on a single gala performance, with orchestra, of an entire silent film. Davis recalls: 'I blithely said: "I've done over 300 clips for this series, why don't we do a complete feature film, with orchestra, and perform it live?" But no one seemed particularly interested.'

'The film suggested to Thames TV was D. W. Griffith's *Broken Blossoms*,' says Kevin Brownlow. 'A very unsympathetic producer glanced at it, and said he thought it would be too corny. We knew then that if we were to convince people we would have to come up with something pile-driving, something that would astonish everyone.'

At the same time the British Film Institute had been working with Kevin Brownlow on a restoration project which had occupied him since he was a boy. 'A major strand in Kevin's life was his obsession with an obscure 1927 French silent film called *Napoléon*,' says Carl Davis. 'It was a "lost" film, which had started out with the aim of covering Napoleon's entire life in six six-hour films. Only Part One was made, but the film keeps growing as more footage comes to light.'

By 1980 Brownlow had assembled a print that ran for nearly five hours. 'I had been restoring this film for years, and it had got to a point where it could conceivably be shown in public. We showed it in rough at the National Film Theatre, just to see how the audience might react. The American Film Institute was planning to open their new theatre in Washington, which would specialise in old movies. The archivist asked if they could have *Napoléon* for their opening film, and said they would pay to have the titles made up. It was shown, accompanied by a cinema organ, and it was a sensation.'

The British Film Institute announced that it would screen the full five-hour version of *Napoléon* at the 24th London International Film Festival in the autumn of 1980, accompanied by a piano. At a party held that summer at the BFI to celebrate the success of the Thames TV *Hollywood* series, at which all the stills and documents amassed during the making of the series were handed over to the BFI's archive, David Gill persuaded Brian Cowgill, managing director of Thames TV, to commission an orchestral score from Carl Davis to accompany the live London screening, in return for Thames securing the TV rights.

'So as our starting point,' says Davis 'we chose the longest, the most difficult, the most ambitious, the most ambiguous and the most dangerous project one could possibly imagine. We were completely inexperienced in this particular field. Nevertheless, on 30 November 1980, at the Empire Theatre in Leicester Square, we embarked on what was intended to be a single performance of *Napoléon*, and without knowing it, we created a legend.'

IV

MUSIC FOR SILENT FILMS

'For all of us involved in the silent film revival,' says Carl Davis, 'the idea of doing a live show was completely unknown territory. My experience as a conductor was principally in a recording studio, where you can repeat things. I was suddenly cast on to the world stage.'

Legend has it that the performance of *Napoléon* at the Empire Theatre in Leicester Square on 30 November 1980 sold out in forty minutes. The British Film Institute immediately decided to mount a further four performances in March 1981. The critics were ecstatic. 'Masterpiece of cinema triumphantly reincarnated,' screamed the headlines. 'An amazing, engrossing, enchanting, dazzling, delightful event,' enthused the film critic of the *Daily Telegraph*. *The Times*' critic Bernard Levin was present at the first performance and subsequently went to see the film three more times, writing in June 1990: 'Abel Gance's film is not just a gigantic, beautiful, daring, original, absorbing, heroic, tremendous and unique masterpiece; it is one of the most completely satisfying and memorable encounters with art I have ever had in my life.'

So what exactly was the appeal of this anachronistic relic of a forgotten era?

The history of *Napoléon*

Napoléon is generally agreed to be the finest work of the French film director and producer Abel Gance (1889–1981). One of the most innovative and ambitious directors of his time, Gance aimed to marry creative integrity with commercial success. The philosophy behind his work bears comparison to that of Richard Wagner, who built his own opera house at Bayreuth with the aim of achieving the ideal *Gesamtkunstwerk*, the Art of the Future, which would unite all aspects of artistic endeavour, visual and auditory, in an all-encompassing spiritual experience. Gance wanted to go one step further. He saw in cinema – 'the music of light' – the possibility of elevating the Art of the Future to a new plane. No longer restricted to the wealthy patrons of a small opera house, it would offer a new kind of inclusive, quasi-religious experience capable of reaching out to millions of people irrespective of nationality, race or social class. The film scholar Dr Paul Cuff considers that 'The greatest exemplar of these ideas is *Napoléon*, a work that marks the apogee of intellectual and aesthetic experimentation in silent cinema.'

Gance had established his own production company, Le Film Français, in 1909, and started off making historical films and psychological melodramas including the 1919 anti-war film *J'accuse*. From the outset, he had a penchant for the colossal – the epic tragedy *Victoire de Samothrace* would have lasted five hours, and *La Roue* (1923), filmed against the background of railway yards, originally ran for nearly nine hours. In the mid 1920s Gance embarked on his most ambitious project – a life of Napoleon Bonaparte in six parts, each lasting about six hours, and ending with the emperor's death on the island of St Helena. Hardly surprisingly, Gance spent his entire budget on Part One, which traces Napoleon's early life. This incorporates his schooldays at the military academy at Brienne-le-Château; his initial endorsement (as a young army lieutenant) of the ideals of the French Revolution (only to be sickened by the random violence of the Terror, and to formulate a desire to bring order to chaos); his return to his native Corsica with the intention of preventing its president from handing the island to the British and his flight by horseback and boat; his heroism during the siege of Toulon; his meeting with Joséphine de Beauharnais, whose husband becomes a victim of the Terror; his and Joséphine's imprisonment during the Terror, from which they are rescued by Robespierre's timely death; his promotion to General in Chief of the Army of the Interior; his marriage to Joséphine; and his plans for the invasion of Italy in 1797. He fills his troops with fighting spirit, and urges them to anticipate the 'honour, glory and riches' which will be theirs if they emerge from the campaign victorious. The film ends with Napoleon reaching the Alps and visualising the glory of future battles, symbolised by the vision of the eagle which he had adopted as a schoolboy and with which he identifies, and by the French tricoloured flag.

'The film is of giant stature, the events in it are of giant stature, the crowds are of giant stature, the battles, the seas, the chases, the Revolution, the Terror, the casting, the actors, the music, are all of giant stature,' wrote Bernard Levin, after seeing the film for the fourth time in 1990. *Napoléon* is packed with a huge cast – which included Albert Dieudonné as Napoleon, Edmond Van Daële as Robespierre, Antonin Artaud as Marat, Gance himself as the young revolutionary leader Saint-Just, who dies with his friend Robespierre on the guillotine, and Gance's wife Marguérite as Marat's murderess, Charlotte Corday. There is no doubt that Dieudonné's charismatic performance in the title-role stole the show. Born in 1889, the same year as Gance, Dieudonné made his acting debut in *L'assassinat du Duc de Guise* (The Murder of the Duke of Guise), the fifteen-minute French silent of 1908 which was one of the first films to feature a specially written musical score, by Camille Saint-Saëns. During the First World War Dieudonné acted in five films directed by Gance, and subsequently appeared in several others under other directors, before being re-hired by Gance to play the lead in his 1927 epic. He identified so closely with Napoleon that he never played another character, and died in 1976, four years before the re-release of the film that made his name.

Napoléon included panoramic historical scenes, recreated in meticulous detail. It was full of experimental techniques, including rapid cutting, the use of hand-held cameras, some attached to horses or mounted on wires, superimposition of images, and some extraordinarily innovative widescreen sequences using a technique called Polyvision. When Gance realised that his original plan of depicting Napoleon's complete life and career was not going to be achieved, he still wanted a spectacular ending. To the amazement of the original audience, the central screen suddenly expanded to three times the size, including two outer panels, with the image filmed on triple cameras, and projected on three machines simultaneously and linked together to make one gigantic picture. The effect was truly sensational, especially when Napoleon was seen riding his horse across the three screens, inspecting his army massed on the Alps before the imminent invasion of Italy, and when a giant eagle – the symbol of Napoleon's destiny – spreads its wings across the screens. Gance's scenario reads: 'A maelstrom fills all three screens. The whole Revolution, swept on at delirious speed toward the heart of Europe, is now one huge tricolor flag, quivering with all that has been inscribed upon it, and it takes on the appearance of an Apocalyptic, tricolor torrent, inundating, enflaming and transfiguring, all at one and the same time.'

Gance's use of his Polyvision technique, far in advance of its time, was not seen again, although it inspired the invention of a process which the Americans bought and named CinemaScope in the 1950s. It did, however, restrict the venues where *Napoléon* could be shown, because there has to be enough room for the two additional screens. The film was first screened in the auditorium of the Paris Opéra on 7 April 1927. There were nine further showings there and elsewhere in Europe, and MGM bought the US rights, but the silent film era was coming to an end and *Napoléon* more or less disappeared. Gance went on to make further films after the arrival first of sound, then of colour, and had considerable influence on French 'New Wave' directors such as François Truffaut. But he did attempt to prolong *Napoléon*'s life by reissuing it in 1935 with dialogue, music and effects, and invented a process similar to stereophonic sound.

The long and painstakingly conducted resurrection of this neglected masterpiece began in 1954, when Kevin Brownlow, then a fifteen-year-old schoolboy, bought two reels of 9.5mm film from a film library in Bromley and screened them on his home projector. Brownlow was entranced by it, later writing in his book on the film: 'The magic of the visuals was especially apparent; the silvery sharpness of the print focused attention on the lighting and the composition. By the time Napoleon had been introduced, in no contrived, theatrical manner, but as an obscure artillery lieutenant on the edge of the crowd, I was in love with the picture. When the action moved to Corsica, and Napoleon was forced to flee, the furious storm at sea intercut with a storm in the Convention made me realise I was watching something exceptional; a film which proved the cinema capable of anything – a film I would have given anything to have made myself.'

Over several decades Brownlow continued to search for long-lost sections of Gance's film, ferreting out extra scenes in archives, flea-markets and film libraries all over the world, and then painstakingly splicing frames and sections together, working at the British Film Institute on the reconstruction of frequently incomplete and damaged sequences. The restoration process was crucial. The footage would have looked wonderful when new, but due to a long period of neglect some of it had decomposed. Eventually a five-hour version emerged, still incomplete, but more closely resembling the original than any of the mutilated versions occasionally shown since the 1920s. This version was first shown in August 1979 at a film festival in Telluride, a mining town in the Rocky Mountains. The film had to be screened in the open air, as there was no indoor screen large enough to accommodate it, and accompanying music was provided by an electronic piano. Abel Gance, then aged 89 and very frail, attended the performance. The mountain air was too cold for him, so he retreated to his hotel room behind the projection area and stood at the window throughout the five-hour showing.

The music for *Napoléon*

During the summer of 1980 a deal was brokered between the new head of the BFI, Anthony Smith, and Brian Cowgill, managing director of Thames Television, to present *Napoléon* at the 24th London Film Festival in November that year. It was to be accompanied not by a piano, as originally planned, but by an orchestral score, so Carl Davis found himself with just over three months to prepare a score for a work of Wagnerian proportions. 'I had to sit down and work out how I was going to put together something of that length, and what its aesthetic approach was going to be,' he says. 'What statement was this score going to make? I felt as if I were stepping into a dead man's shoes. But I remembered my conversation with the cinema organist Ann Leaf when we were making the *Hollywood* series, and what she had told me about how to construct a silent movie score from existing material.'

The music which originally accompanied *Napoléon* was composed by Arthur Honegger, who also acted as musical director for the first performance at the Paris Opéra. About twenty-five minutes of it was original; the rest of the music consisted of extracts from Beethoven symphonies, and pieces by Haydn, Mozart, Massenet, Franck, Litolff, Méhul and Tchaikovsky. Honegger also had a choir, soloists and actors to read Napoleon's speeches, as well as an orchestra at his disposal. Unfortunately only fragments of the Honegger score survive, although memoirs of the performance exist. 'Honegger had several themes – a Napoleon theme and a Joséphine theme, for instance – that were repeated,' says Davis. 'He had a very good march – his own arrangement of Méhul's *Le chant du départ*, a war song which was composed in 1794 and became the official anthem of Napoleon's First Empire. Honegger used it for the liberation of Italy, in counterpoint to the *Marseillaise*.

'But all that didn't help me very much. I knew I couldn't write five hours-worth of original music for *Napoléon* in three months: that would be suicidal. But if I could *find* appropriate music, as they did in the silent movie years, the choices I made could be creative in their own right, and would introduce another level. Because time was so short, I started to work with orchestrators, which I hadn't done before. I met Christopher Palmer, one of the finest symphonic orchestrators of his generation, and a passionate devotee of film music. He was trained by Miklós Rózsa, and had worked with Bernard Herrmann. Christopher introduced me to the Matthews brothers, David and Colin, both composers who were then at the outset of their careers and eager to get more experience in arrangement and orchestration. We played games – I asked them to re-orchestrate pieces in the styles of other composers. They did astonishing arrangements and orchestration, they were spot on.'

'Working on *Napoléon* became all-encompassing because it was such a huge project,' says Colin Matthews. 'David and I came in at a relatively late stage – we were thrown at it and given various bits to do. It was a huge learning curve for all of us. It was the first time Carl had done anything like that, and indeed the first time anyone had done anything of that enormous scope. Carl had to learn on the job how to sustain this huge score, and at that stage it was a question of him finding out what we could do. The pressure was all on him: he occasionally got worked up, and the atmosphere could get fraught, because everybody was learning. But his dedication to the job was immense, and we had nothing but admiration for his technique.'

'From a compositional point of view, it is like composing a huge ballet or an opera,' says Davis. 'The score has been described as acting as a bridge – the music is the bridge between today's public and the anachronistic style of silent film, where people seem to speak but you don't hear what they are saying, and scenes are constantly interrupted with title-cards bearing text. The score must make sense of a stream of images, without any dialogue.'

'Film scores are written in short sections,' says David Matthews. 'Carl would give me a run of sections, and would then play them through to me on the piano. We would discuss the orchestration – he had quite clear ideas about what he wanted. So I started with a piano score with orchestral indications, and I had to turn it into an orchestral score. I would add bits if I thought that the piano texture was too thin. I enjoyed filling it out – it involved me in a bit of composing as well as just arranging. The experience of writing for an orchestra that I gained through working with Carl on his film scores was a very valuable one. I think it's fair to say that my skill as an arranger grew out of my work with Carl, and arranging is now a major part of my life as a composer.'

'We just had the video without any time-codes,' says Colin Matthews. 'Carl sat with a stop-watch, going through the whole film. Everything had to be timed; it was an incredible labour, and a very arduous process. Carl lived in Streatham then, and we went over to see him regularly. He played through the score on the piano with the film. We didn't have our own copies at that stage. We would take away a piano score, marked with fairly clear instructions as to what Carl wanted. We worked in substantial chunks. David and I each did about two hundred pages of scoring. Carl did a small amount himself, but there just wasn't time for that as well as composing. The time-scale for *Napoléon* and indeed all the subsequent silent movies was so compressed – he had to write unremittingly, and had no time to score. Originally in the film world they would have used orchestrators, it was very common. Carl was perfectly capable of orchestrating himself, but he wanted the extra element that we could bring to it.'

David Matthews considers that, generally speaking, it is hard to distinguish his own style of orchestration from that of his brother – the changeover between them is seamless. But, based on their own individual compositional styles, Carl Davis thinks of David as the romantic, and tends to allocate love scenes to him, whereas Colin's personal style is more astringent. One of the most striking passages of orchestration in *Napoléon* comes in the scene after the Terror has come to an end. Napoleon enters the empty National Assembly Hall and sees the ghosts of dead Revolutionary figures: Danton, Marat, Robespierre and Saint-Just. Davis asked Colin Matthews to pretend that he was Webern or Schoenberg, and to give Beethoven's C minor Piano Variations a ghostly twist. 'He asked me for something very spooky and gave me the outline,' says Colin. 'The first thing I learned was not to make things too complicated, because Carl sometimes asked for very elaborate orchestrations. I overdid the ghost scene at first, as we subsequently realised that it was something that couldn't easily be rehearsed. That was the big learning curve, how to write film music that an orchestra could come in and sight-read. Working with Carl, I learned so much in terms of orchestration, having not known before how to tackle something like a silent film score. It simplified my own orchestral style to some extent, but I learned how to do tricks that sounded so much more complicated than they actually were.'

'I had to work out an overall approach,' says Davis. 'The score for *Napoléon* had to tell its own story. Could the music not tell a story of Napoleon's time? I have always been interested in music history, and I already had a vast repertoire to hand. I chose to focus on the composers who were in some way related to Napoleon. For a start I would use some Beethoven – some of it well known, some less familiar, such as his *Rule Britannia* variations. There is a good match between Beethoven and Napoleon. Throughout the film, you are impressed by Napoleon's dynamism, the intensity of his feelings and the directness of his actions. This could be a description of certain qualities in Beethoven's music.'

The *Napoléon* score is marinaded in Beethoven. Davis took as his starting point the composer tearing up his original dedication of the *Eroica* Symphony to Napoleon, furious that a man who had formerly seemed to embody Enlightenment ideals had declared himself Emperor. He dedicated it instead to one of his own aristocratic patrons, adding that it was intended 'to celebrate the memory of a great man'. Davis also recalls the account of Beethoven, a few years later, huddling under a table in his apartment in Vienna, while Napoleon's cannons were pounding the city. 'I wanted to give the impression that Beethoven himself was scoring the film. Looking closely at Beethoven made me realise his gifts as an orchestrator. I could take the theme of the *Eroica* Symphony as a starting point; but then there were all the uses that Beethoven made of the *Eroica* material – the "Eroica" piano variations, the finale of the *Prometheus* ballet, the contredanses. Scenes where Napoleon is on horseback could be set to the scherzo from the *Eroica* Symphony.'

A masterly Beethovenian mash-up, using parts of the storm movement from the 'Pastoral' Symphony, as well as sections of the *Coriolan* Overture, accompanies the celebrated 'Double Storm' sequence, in which Napoleon is trying to escape from Corsica by boat during a storm at sea, cross-cut with equally stormy scenes of violent disagreement at a meeting of the Convention in Revolutionary Paris. The cinematic effects were extraordinarily innovative and exceptionally realistic – the hall where the Convention is meeting begins to swing from side to side to match the mountainous waves pummelling Napoleon's boat (Dieudonné, playing Napoleon, was genuinely terrified) – and the music intensifies the drama. Davis also uses a particularly macabre piece from a late Beethoven string quartet to accompany the scene during the Terror where members of the Convention are preparing dossiers to decide who is going to be sent to the guillotine.

'*Napoléon* incorporated a lot of pre-existing music,' says Colin Matthews. 'There was some literal cutting and pasting from Beethoven's work, but the extracts couldn't run on for too long, so we worked on re-scoring some of it. There were a number of elaborations of Beethoven, not just the orchestral music, but piano pieces and string quartets, and the Variations on "Rule, Britannia", which Carl later asked me to orchestrate in its entirety. It was an obvious thing to base the score on music of the period: Mozart's early G minor Symphony No. 25 accompanies the snowball fight among the young cadets at the Brienne-le-Château military academy at the beginning of the film.'

'[Davis] . . . has ransacked Haydn, Mozart and above all Beethoven, and fitted their work to his so skilfully that the seams are truly imperceptible. On an ocean of C major the silent film floats, sounding depths and breadths that anyone would have thought impossible in a two-dimensional medium,' wrote Bernard Levin.

'I think it was a stroke of genius to select composers who were alive at the same time as Napoleon,' says Kevin Brownlow. 'The sets and costumes are all perfectly appropriate to the period, but the music lends it an uncanny authenticity.'

'Historically,' says Carl Davis, 'these composers didn't exist in a vacuum. They were part of society, and they were affected in various ways by what was happening during the Napoleonic period. It was all interrelated. I also wanted to make sure that French composers, or those working in France at the time, would be represented – Cherubini, Méhul, Gossec – they are a step down the musical ladder now, but were very well thought of in their time, and their music is charming. It became really very interesting to work on music that rarely gets heard – overtures by Cherubini, Monsigny, and Grétry.' Their work inspired the dance pieces such as the minuet, gigue and tambourin that Davis used for the *Bal des victimes*, at which Napoleon and Joséphine finally meet and fall in love. Two of those dances, the gigue and the tambourin, are lively, brassy and uninhibited, while the central piece, *The Fan*, is more decorous – a delicately scored, waltz-like minuet featuring solo violin and flute, derived from an early Mozart minuet.

Napoleon is known to have said that he could listen to an aria from Paisiello's opera *Nina* every day of his life, and Davis used that melody to accompany a scene in Part One set in Corsica, where Napoleon and his sister are visiting their mother at the family home, and have a picnic. Corsican folk-songs, including a lament, play a major part in the score to represent peaceful scenes of rural life. When Napoleon is forced to flee on horseback from Calvi, his headlong flight is accompanied by a brilliant tarantella, played on high woodwind and underscored by an insistent drumbeat. Davis also made use of a hurdy-gurdy. 'It's seen being played during the film, so I thought, "Let's find the real thing." Doreen Muskett, an expert on the hurdy-gurdy, and the author of a manual on how to play it, came to me with a volume of eighteenth-century dances arranged for the instrument. I grabbed about four of those tunes immediately, because they were absolutely suited to the instrument, and I thought its chilling buzz would effectively underline the cold, pitiless character of Robespierre.

'The French Revolution itself is integrated into the Napoleon story, so there was all the material from that period. What were the popular songs that people sang? I looked at the first printed settings of the songs from the French Revolution, such as *La Marseillaise, La Carmagnole* and the *Ça ira!* and preserved these in their original form. Generally speaking, I gave myself an end-date of 1810, beyond which I wouldn't take any music. There's one piece, however, that is well outside the Napoleonic period – Bach's C minor Passacaglia. I reserved that for one particular character – the implacable Saint-Just, the Stalin of his age.

'The film had a particular, romanticised outlook on the events it deals with, and that's where my love of classic literature came in. I wanted to tell the story through the music of the late eighteenth century. Whenever I felt the director's view became subjective, rather than strictly historical, my original music takes over. The most important is the Eagle theme – representing the actual young eagle that Napoleon keeps caged at school, and which returns voluntarily to him after it is freed – and it also represents Destiny, a symbol of Napoleon's spirit.'

The 'Eagle of Destiny' theme, which recurs throughout the film, is one of Davis's most majestic creations. 'Carl's Eagle theme is just fantastic,' says Kevin Brownlow. A variant of the four-note motif that opens the finale of the 'Eroica' Symphony, it is first heard on a solo horn, but at climactic points blazes out triumphantly with the full weight of the brass section behind it. Together with the *Marseillaise* and material drawn directly from Beethoven's symphonies, it is threaded throughout the score like a Wagnerian *Leitmotif*, and is subjected to development in the manner of classical symphonies. Towards the end of the film it swells triumphantly as a title announces: 'And in the sky, a strange conductor beats out the rhythms of the army', and the eagle spreads its wings across the triple screen. As the screens turn the colours of the French flag, and images from Napoleon's past and future converge over a background of fire, sun, and water, the Destiny theme merges in counterpoint with those of his twin passions: the romantic theme associated with Joséphine, and the *Marseillaise*, the aural symbol of his patriotic spirit. 'Davis weaves these musical aspects together, elevating the entire work to the heights of French Romantic, sweeping, grand opera,' commented one critic after a 2014 screening of *Napoléon* in Holland.

'*Napoléon* has few love scenes,' says Colin Matthews. 'There is one scene where Napoleon is contemplating conquering the world. He looks at a globe, and he sees Joséphine's face looking out at him, superimposed on the map of the world. Carl turned that into a love scene. That was wonderful. Otherwise there would have been nothing like that in the film – his music added a completely new dimension. It was a very clever thing to do.'

The screening of *Napoléon*

Brownlow, Gill and Davis knew that they were taking a huge risk with the screening of *Napoléon* with a live orchestra – in this case, the 47-piece Wren Orchestra of London. In rehearsal, if the orchestra and the images got out of sync, the reel could simply be rewound and they could start again. But that was not going to be possible at the performance. 'That day changed everything,' says Davis. 'I had to learn how to assemble the existing musical material, edit it, compose new music and attempt to synchronise it to the film. I had, in short, to acquire the skills of an opera or ballet conductor – only instead of singers and dancers, I had the inflexibility of the screen. I realised that the secret all lay in tempi. I knew that if I had conceived a piece to fit in a certain tempo, I had to hit that tempo to keep in sync.'

When Davis had worked with Brownlow and Gill on the *Hollywood* series, he learned that most screenings of silent films are projected too fast. There was no standard speed for silent films, and as cameras were originally hand-cranked, the speed of the action depended on how fast or how slowly the crank was turned. Turning it too slowly produces the jerky, speeded-up effect that many people associate with black-and-white silent movies. Carl Davis says, 'My colleagues were deeply concerned about all this, and when it came to looking at correct speeds, it was very important that decisions about this were made before I composed the music, because if I wanted the score to synchronise, the projection speed had to be stable. The projectors had to be attached to variable speed mechanisms.'

Before the tickets for *Napoléon* went on sale, an official at the British Film Institute remarked gloomily that he doubted that there would be more than about 200 people at the performance. Kevin Brownlow was astonished to arrive at the Empire Theatre to find queues of people waiting outside, and up to £100 being offered for a ticket. 'I remember coming out of the Underground absolutely terrified. The film lasted four hours and fifty minutes, and I thought, "Who's going to sit through a silent film for that long?" Then I thought the orchestra would never keep in sync, and I realised that if the audience rejected it, that would be the end of my long love-affair with this film.' Carl Davis was equally nervous. 'In a sense this was my first live appearance as a conductor, and certainly the first time that anyone had appeared since the 1920s conducting a full orchestra with a score that was synchronised with the film – and with zero experience!'

Miraculously, everything came together. 'I got everything to work, and the orchestra found they had taken on a score as long as the longest Wagner opera – in fact, one of the French reviews described *Napoléon* as "un opéra sans voix" (an opera without voices). There were conveniently placed intervals, but otherwise they were playing more or less non-stop for just under five hours,' says Davis. Brownlow later recalled in his book on the film: 'Carl Davis's synchronisation was heroic – almost uncanny. Again and again, as the film faded out, so did the music. The sparks flew from the anvil in the Danton sequence – he had incorporated an anvil into the orchestra. Cannons fired – the percussion was often simultaneous. But quite beyond my powers of description was what he had done with the music to raise the picture to an emotional peak I had never experienced at any of the other screenings.'

'The reaction of the audience was staggering,' recalls Brownlow. 'It caught them in the first two reels – the scenes at the cadet college in Brienne, the way the boy Napoleon is treated, and the pet eagle. I always say that if you don't react to that film by the end of Reel Two, then you might as well leave the theatre. So far I've found just three people out of the thousands who've seen it who really dislike it, and one of those was suffering from flu when she saw it.'

Everyone present on that memorable day was thrilled by the immersive experience of Live Cinema, of being surrounded by thousands of people who gasped, laughed and applauded. 'The experience was astonishing,' says Colin Matthews. 'You could literally feel the audience's reaction. The show lasted from 10 a.m. until 5 p.m., and the first horn player was going on to do Mahler's Eighth Symphony in the evening!'

'There were thousands of people there,' says Jeremy Isaacs. 'The house came down with joy, amazement and congratulations, and the principal figure who made this happen was Carl. After the performance, I went backstage to congratulate the "Mega-Maestro", as I jokingly called him, and his beautiful white shirt was wringing with sweat, because of the sheer physical effort he had to put into it.' Mamoun Hassan, later to become Head of the BFI Production Board, summed up the enthusiastic response to the screening in a letter to Kevin Brownlow: 'It was not only that the film was unique – a masterpiece like no other – but also that the occasion itself revived the basic experience of cinema which has almost been lost; a *community* of experience. At the end we were clapping and cheering the film, Gance, you, the composer and the orchestra, but also ourselves. We had seen so much, felt so much and given so much.'

The critics were certainly won over. Writing in the *Daily Telegraph*, Eric Shorter singled out Davis's score for plaudits: 'No wonder the house rose with a roar of gratitude at every pause in the day's proceedings. For it may not be a marvel to accompany a five-hour silent film on the piano. But how often has an orchestra of this scale and quality done so with such exhilarating charm, precision, and discreet sympathy?'

One of Colin Matthews's most enduring memories from that day was of Kevin Brownlow appearing on stage at the end, holding up a phone to enable the ninety-one-year-old Abel Gance in Paris to hear the rapturous applause and cheers of the London audience. Brownlow admits that the greatest regret is that Gance never saw *Napoléon* with Carl's music. 'He was very musical, he made a film about Beethoven. He would have responded to the music like no one else.'

'For me,' Gance had written in 1974, 'a spectator who maintains his critical sense is not a spectator. I wanted the audience to emerge from the theatre amazed victims, completely won over, returning to the squalor of earth from paradise. *That* is cinema!'

Gance died in November 1981. A year later, *Napoléon* was performed in France with Davis's score, to ecstatic press reviews. It had two performances at the Maison de la Culture in Le Havre with the Wren Orchestra to a ten-minute standing ovation. 'Le Havre was incredible,' says Kevin Brownlow. 'It was a wonderful screening in a wonderful theatre, and at the end the huge wide screen rose up, allowing the audience to see all the projectors and the technicians behind it.' Six months later, accompanied by the Orchestre Colonne, *Napoléon* had its Paris premiere at the Palais des Congrès, a huge venue seating about four thousand people. Carl Davis says that the first Paris performance was particularly moving. 'At the end of the first performance, a *défilé* of people, including several of the actors who had actually worked on Gance's original film, came on stage.' The French Government was so enthusiastic about the film that in 1983 both Carl Davis and Kevin Brownlow were made Chevaliers de l'Ordre des Arts et des Lettres, in recognition of their contribution to French culture.

The colossal success of *Napoléon* generated an avalanche of interest in the revival of silent films with live orchestral accompaniment. It was shown all round the world. Different countries had their 'cinemathèques' – the French in Paris, the Germans in Munich – but before 1980 showings of silent films were very specialised. Suddenly *Napoléon* was selling out huge halls – venues such as the 2,400-seat Royal Festival Hall and the Barbican in London. 'It kick-started a revival of interest in the repertoire,' says Davis. 'It went to Strasbourg, Lausanne, Luxembourg, Helsinki, Tel-Aviv, Athens, to Italy for the Pordenone Festival, then more recently, to San Francisco and the

Holland Festival in Amsterdam.' A cut-down, three-and-a-half hour version for the US market with a score by Carmine Coppola emerged in 1981, and was premiered in Radio City Music Hall in New York in front of an audience of 6000.

Brownlow re-edited *Napoléon* in 2000, incorporating 35 minutes of previously missing footage that had been found in the Cinémathèque Française in Paris. The total length of the restored film, shown at its original speed of 20 frames per second, now runs to more than five and a half hours. This version was screened four times, with the Oakland East Bay Symphony conducted by Davis, at the Paramount Theatre in Oakland, California, at the end of March 2012. The most recent UK performance of the revised version took place on 30 November 2013 at the Royal Festival Hall, with the Philharmonia Orchestra conducted by Davis. Including intervals and a dinner break, it took eight hours altogether, and received an enthusiastic standing ovation. Its many admirers all over the world would concur with Bernard Levin's assessment: 'Napoléon is . . . an artistic creation that can never be forgotten, and will endure as long as art does.'

The Thames Silents

As Jeremy Isaacs, who was in the process of setting up the new Channel 4 TV network, was leaving the crowded foyer of the Empire Cinema, a woman called across to him: 'Jeremy, are you going to put *Napoléon* on Channel 4?' He replied: "If *Napoléon* doesn't appear on Channel 4, there's no point in having a Channel 4." And indeed, the film was screened on the new channel in 1983.

'Everybody had proclaimed that the *Hollywood* series was pointing to the importance of silent movies as part of our cultural heritage, something that we should continue to support and enjoy,' says Isaacs. 'Somebody asked the bright question of Thames TV: "You guys have done this series, it's very good, you have a lot of money, why don't you spend some money each year on presenting a major silent movie in the cinema, with a live orchestra?" So I announced that via Thames TV, Channel 4 would commission David Gill and Kevin Brownlow to produce versions of the great masterpieces of the silent film era, with the understanding that Carl would write the scores.' Their premieres, with live orchestra, would be given in one of three major London cinemas – the Empire in Leicester Square, the Dominion in Tottenham Court Road, or the London Palladium – at the annual London Film Festival in October. 'David and Carl thought it would be a great idea to put these silent films back in the theatre with an orchestra, as they would have been seen originally,' says Kevin Brownlow. 'It would be like a new form of entertainment, as you would have needed to be at least ninety years old to have seen any of them first time round.'

'I stuck with the commitment I had made to commission an annual silent movie with live orchestral accompaniment, and it meant that by splitting the cost with Thames, they paid for the making of the film itself, and we at Channel 4 paid for the conductor and the musicians,' says Jeremy Isaacs. 'All the films were very individual. Carl wrote the music, and never got one wrong. That speaks of great breadth of musical knowledge and a huge technical gift. The Thames Silents were a tremendous success, and thanks to some very positive thinking within the company, they got the credit for it, even though they didn't want to put them on TV. If you were running a commercial channel, putting a long silent movie on screen, maybe lasting over two hours, would be a very difficult thing to do.'

'David Gill immediately approached the major studios who owned the prints and rights of silent films,' says Carl Davis, 'and started licensing an enormous amount of material, beginning with nine films from the MGM catalogue. He went to Paramount, he went to Harold Lloyd's granddaughter Suzanne, and to Raymond Rohauer, the copyright holders of the entire Buster Keaton catalogue, as well as those of Douglas Fairbanks and Rudolph Valentino. Kevin and David came up with a grand master-scheme looking years ahead. It was exclusively about Hollywood films at that point, and it was to be as varied as possible – it would include romantic films starring people like Valentino, Douglas Fairbanks and Garbo; it had epics like *Intolerance* and *Ben-Hur*, fantasies like *The Thief of Bagdad*. It would have an element of Westerns, it would take in comedies, war films like *The Big Parade* and *Wings*, that in 1928 won the first Academy Award for Best Picture; and it would take in one-offs, like *Greed* and *The Crowd*.'

'People were thrilled to bits,' says Kevin Brownlow. 'At last, many of the classics of silent cinema (unavailable for so long) and some unknown films were being seen again.

'Everyone had said how fantastic *Napoléon* was, but that we would never find another silent film to follow it,' continues Brownlow. 'So in 1981, for the first of the Thames Silents, we chose one that was the complete opposite, an intimate epic, very downbeat. But it filled the Empire Theatre and the Royal Festival Hall.' Set in New York, the plot of King Vidor's 1928 film *The Crowd* concerns an ambitious man who works for an insurance firm as a clerk, and wants to get on and live the American Dream, but is frustrated. The film deals in a highly realistic way with pre-Depression-era social deprivation and unemployment, and is said to have influenced the Italian post-war neo-realist movement.

Davis had already composed music for some sequences for *The Crowd* in the *Hollywood* series. 'Now I got to do the complete film. It's very sophisticated.' Kevin Brownlow recalls he was astounded by Carl's powerful score.

'Year by year we added to the catalogue, mostly one film per year, sometimes as many as three,' says Davis. 'I felt I was a one-man opera company. How long it takes me to write a score for a silent depends on length. For a film lasting around 90 minutes, I usually allowed myself about three months to write the score. You are associated with visual media, and it's important not to get into complex orchestral textures. They are simply not heard. You're in the business of making an immediate impact. The audience has to feel informed as to what's going on, in a very direct way, and if it's too subtle, with too many things going on, it doesn't work. I found the best way to tackle this was to write fast. As a general principle, it's "How much time have I got?" Film tends to be a slave to a deadline. The first deadline is the dub, when all the sound elements are put together. The dialogue, the sound effects and the music are all welded into a single experience. In London there's a dearth of dubbing suites. I found very quickly that you had to book your space early, and then everything has to conform to that date. You just can't miss that deadline. Technologically we're now in a different world where you no longer need to book one of the largest studios in London to make an orchestra sound big. Digitalisation has produced miniaturisation. Everything is smaller and more focused. When I started, they still did editing with sticky tape and a razor blade, losing bits of film if you dropped it on the floor. Now, with the Avid editing system with multi-screens, you don't handle any physical material at all.'

Carl Davis says that from the start of his collaboration with Gill, Brownlow and Thames TV on the silent film repertoire, it seemed clear that their first objective was to get the films shown on TV, but the next would be to get them released on (at that time) home video, then eventually on DVD. But with *Napoléon*, he says, 'we had breached the barrier of live performance with orchestra, and suddenly, a genre that had not existed since the 1920s, Live Cinema, seemed red-hot. All the scores I did had the twin objective, first of making a product for broadcast or home consumption, and at the same time, being able to perform them live.'

'Suddenly everyone was taking these films absolutely seriously, after a long period when they'd been parodied and belittled, and shown – if at all – with a honky-tonk piano. Now they seemed like operas,' says Kevin Brownlow.

Carl Davis agrees. 'Silent films are a unique form when they are presented orchestrally. In one sense they're like opera or ballet, in that you're going to see a spectacle. Adding the live element to film presents you with something different, not like anything else. The best silent movies are coherent films with sophisticated plotting, great stories, great camerawork and great acting. You accept their conventions as you would in an opera by Monteverdi or Mozart.'

Over the decade following the November 1980 premiere of *Napoléon*, thirteen silent films from the Brownlow–Gill–Davis partnership were premiered with live orchestra under the aegis of Thames TV, mostly in London. Two – *Greed* and *Intolerance* – were premiered respectively in Edinburgh and Leeds. The last in the initial sequence, Raymond Bernard's 1927 historical epic *The Chess Player*, had an original score by Henri Rabaud, for which Carl Davis discovered a missing scene indicated in the published score, and worked on the synchronisation.

After 1990, Thames TV commissioned several more silents with Davis's scores, but more sporadically, and the live premieres generally took place at European film festivals. Among these was *A Woman of Affairs*, a tragic story of thwarted love starring Greta Garbo and her real-life lover John Gilbert, directed by Clarence Brown. Liszt's Petrarch Sonnet No. 123, from Book II of the *Années de pélèrinage*, weaves through the score like a *Leitmotif*. The piano on the 1995 recording is played by Ian Hobson, who won the 1981 Leeds International Piano Competition. Another, premiered in Luxembourg the following year, was *The Student Prince in Old Heidelberg*, directed in 1927 by Ernst Lubitsch, starring Ramon Novarro and Norma Shearer. David Matthews, who has worked with Carl Davis on twelve silents, beginning with *Napoléon* and *The Crowd*, says that *Old Heidelberg*, the bitter-sweet story of a romance between a crown prince and an innkeeper's daughter, was his favourite collaboration. 'It was beautifully filmed. I orchestrated the entire score in the space of a month. It ran to 600 pages of full score – I don't quite know how I did it. I was working flat out, fourteen hours a day. The score is very romantic. Carl took Wagner's *Die Meistersinger* as his model.' Kevin Brownlow recalls that *Old Heidelberg* was first shown at the National Film Theatre in London accompanied by a piano, to an audience of about twenty-five people. 'Taking a risk, we put it into the London Film Festival at the Royal Festival Hall with Carl's score, and over 2000 people turned up!'

Carl Davis says that in the first instance, the film scores would be recorded in the studio shortly after their Live Cinema premieres, with the same orchestra. 'The initial performances of *Napoléon* and several others were done by the Wren Orchestra, but then, when I spread my wings and decided to use some of the other London orchestras, we had the phenomenon of the English Chamber Orchestra premiering *The Big Parade* in 1984 and recording several of the films. The Philharmonia, which had already invited me to give several concerts, recorded *The Thief of Bagdad*, and the London Philharmonic Orchestra recorded *Ben-Hur*, and gave five performances of it at the London Palladium in 1987. The London Symphony and London Philharmonic Orchestras, as well as the Philharmonia, have performed and recorded many of the films.

'In the twenty years since I had come to England in 1960, I had amassed a great deal of experience in the studio, and was able to treat a silent film as if it were a contemporary feature film. The score could be broken down into segments. In the old days you would have had your standard orchestra, with standardised musical treatments, whereas we now had the protected circumstances of a studio orchestra, and we had the time to treat each film individually on its merit. Each film had its own specific sound. If it was a big romantic film or an epic, it needed a big orchestra with a lot of strings. I'm currently working on a Valentino film called *The Son of the Sheik*, which is set in Algeria. Reading about the musical culture of North Africa makes me realise that it's made up of so many sources, a mixture of Arabic, Middle Eastern and Spanish music. When the Moors were expelled from Spain in 1492 they took elements of Spanish culture with them. Then there's another overlay, from the French colonial occupation. The film itself is set in 1925, the year it was made. The French were still there, so elements of French cabaret music creep in. If you were in Morocco, for instance, that would be more associated with the Africa of the desert, but Algerian music has a very strong French flavour. By that process, you put together an instrumental ensemble that specifically belongs to that film.

Carl collecting a BAFTA lifetime achievement award, 2003

THE BRITISH FILM INSTITUTE

NAPO

VU PAR ABEL GANCE

A NEWLY RESTORED PRINT

SCORE CREATED AND CONDUCTED

BY CARL DAVIS

SATURDAY 3 JUNE 2000

2.30PM - 10.30PM ROYAL FESTIVAL HALL

Royal Festival Hall
Queen Elizabeth Hall
Purcell Room

Carl in rehearsal at the Pordenone Silent Film Festival in 2016
(Photograph: Valerio Greco)

Channel Four Silents presents LIVE CINEMA

Ben Asquith's

THE FOUR HORSEMEN
OF THE APOCALYPSE

starring RUDOLPH VALENTINO

The Live Cinema Orchestra.
Music composed and
conducted by CARL DAVIS

Camden Parkway Cinema
Fri 20 Sep Sun 23 Nov 1992
Box office 071 267 7034
CC First Call (24 hr) 071 240 7200

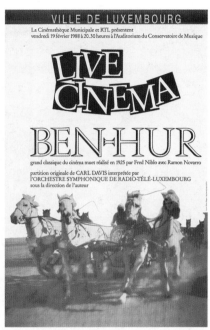

La Cinémathèque Municipale et RTL présentent
vendredi 19 février 1988 à 20.30 heures à l'Auditorium du Conservatoire de Musique

LIVE CINEMA

BEN-HUR

grand classique du cinéma muet réalisé en 1925 par Fred Niblo avec Ramon Novarro

partition originale de CARL DAVIS interprétée par
l'ORCHESTRE SYMPHONIQUE DE RADIO-TÉLÉ-LUXEMBOURG
sous la direction de l'auteur

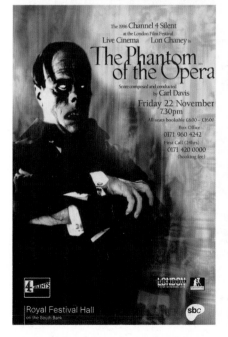

The 1996 Channel 4 Silent
at the London Film Festival
Live Cinema   Lon Chaney is

The Phantom
of the Opera

Score composed and conducted
by Carl Davis

Friday 22 November
7.30pm

All seats bookable £6.00 – £16.00

Box Office
0171 960 4242
First Call (24hrs)
0171 420 0000
(booking fee)

Royal Festival Hall
on the South Bank

John Gilbert
in King Vidor's
The Big Parade

Cinema-Teatro Verdi, Pordenone, 3 ottobre 1987 - ore 21.00
Orchestra Sinfonica della Radiotelevisione di Lubiana diretta da Carl Davis

(MGM, 1925)

A moment in history captured by the sword and the heart.

THE FAR PAVILIONS
AN EPIC ADVENTURE

HOME BOX OFFICE PREMIERE FILMS' PRESENTS A GEOFFREY REEVE PRODUCTION FOR GOLDCREST
THE FAR PAVILIONS BEN CROSS AMY IRVING OMAR SHARIF
JOHN GIELGUD ROSSANO BRAZZI AND CHRISTOPHER LEE
DIRECTOR OF PHOTOGRAPHY JACK CARDIFF SCREENPLAY BY JULIAN BOND BASED ON THE NOVEL BY M.M. KAYE
MUSIC BY CARL DAVIS DIRECTED BY PETER DUFFELL PRODUCED BY GEOFFREY REEVE EXECUTIVE PRODUCER JOHN PEVERALL

HBO
Premiere Films

King Vidor's **The Crowd** (USA 1928)

Live Cinema

Musique de
Carl Davis
Orchestre
Philharmonique
du Luxembourg

sous la direction de
Carl Davis

Avant-programme
Charlie Chaplin's THE CURE
(USA 1918)
Première mondiale de la
nouvelle musique de
Carl Davis

16 et 17 mars 2001 à 20.00 h
au Conservatoire de Musique
de la Ville de Luxembourg
Prévente Billetterie Centrale

Organisé par la Cinémathèque
de la Ville de Luxembourg

En collaboration avec l'OPL
Avec le concours de
Photoplay Productions Ltd.,
Faber Music Ltd.,
Threefold Music

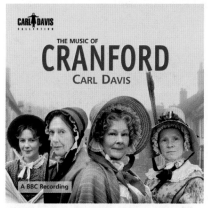

THE MUSIC OF
CRANFORD
CARL DAVIS

A BBC Recording

FULL SCORE

PRIDE AND PREJUDICE
SUITE FOR SMALL ORCHESTRA
Music from the award-winning BBC dramatization
of Jane Austen's novel
CARL DAVIS

FABER *ff* MUSIC

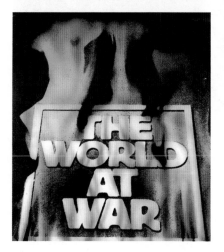

THE WORLD AT WAR

David Gill, Carl Davis and Kevin Brownlow

The *Hollywood* team – Thames Television

'In *The Son of the Sheik* we have a stunning star in Valentino, who is still fascinating to watch; a plot from a best-selling novel which was both erotic and exotic, and there's a lot of dancing in it, because the leading lady belongs to a troupe of street performers. She was a Hungarian actress called Vilma Banky, she was blonde and blue eyed (very improbably) but she was a good dancer and an effective actress. All these elements are in my score.

'Every one of the productions is unique from a musical point of view. For instance, if we were working on a film contemporary to the 1920s, it might have a strong jazz element. *The Thief of Bagdad*, which starred Douglas Fairbanks as an Arabian thief who rescues a princess, has lots of fantastic special effects like a flying carpet. It reminded me so forcibly of a Ballets Russes production, with its Slavic Orientalism, that I restricted my borrowings almost entirely to Rimsky-Korsakov, both *Scheherezade* and the little-known opera *The Invisible City of Kitezh*. My own orchestration jumped a mile when I began to use pieces by Rimsky-Korsakov, because one had to look at how certain effects were achieved.' Kevin Brownlow thinks that Davis's choice of Rimsky-Korsakov for *The Thief of Bagdad* was another stroke of genius. 'When we sent it mute to the publicity department, the initial reaction was "What are we going to do with this, it's really boring." Then we put it on live with Carl's huge orchestra, and afterwards the publicity man came up saying: "That was fantastic!" The element of risk is tremendous, as most of these films had fallen into oblivion. However big the stars were, we had to work very hard on the publicity front.'

For Clarence Brown's *The Eagle*, again starring Rudolph Valentino and Vilma Banky, and based on a Pushkin story set in Russia in the time of Catherine the Great, Davis devised a Russian-sounding score, with echoes of Rimsky-Korsakov, Borodin and Tchaikovsky. Another Valentino classic, *The Four Horseman of the Apocalypse*, begins in Argentina and ends on the European battlefields of World War I, and contains an emblematic moment when Valentino dances a sexy tango, accompanied by swooning violins, a cornet solo, and castanets. But the film, with its anti-war message, really deals with struggle and catastrophe, underlined by Davis's quotations from Liszt's *Après une lecture de Dante*. 'Carl's music gave *The Four Horsemen of the Apocalypse* a completely new lease of life,' says Kevin Brownlow. 'It was such a powerful experience. Nobody tittered at Valentino like they used to do.'

Erich von Stroheim's *The Wedding March* is set in Vienna in the closing days of the Habsburg Empire, so Davis's 1998 score for that uses themes by the Viennese masters, including Schubert and Johann Strauss II. Films with more contemporary subject matter on the other hand, such as *It*, the 1927 comedy starring Clara Bow as a sales assistant in a department store who schemes to marry her boss, make use of the jazzy dance idioms of the 1920s.

'Another very interesting example', says Davis, 'was D. W. Griffith's epic film *Intolerance*, released in 1916. It's a pacifist film, but America was just on the edge of entering the First World War when it was released. It failed at the time because most films of that period were aggressively patriotic, encouraging people to support America's entry into the war.' That film has four inter-cut episodes set in contrasting periods, each dealing with an aspect of intolerance, and scored for contrasting ensembles in appropriate styles. A lush, exotic, neo-Richard Straussian score for full orchestra accompanies the destruction of Babylon; the massacre of the Huguenots utilises a Renaissance-sounding ensemble with recorder and lute; the crucifixion of Jesus is set to a Baroque-sounding score; and the fourth tableau, a contemporary story involving the rescue of a boy from being hanged, is scored for a small theatre orchestra. 'Each film has a different model for its orchestration,' says David Matthews, 'and Carl and I would always discuss the style. For exotic subjects like *Ben-Hur* and the Babylon scene in *Intolerance*, we decided that we would go for a decadent, *fin de siècle* kind of sound.' Kevin Brownlow is of the opinion that there is no more difficult film to accompany than *Intolerance*. 'Four different stories, all running together. Carl gave each story its own character and brought it all together in a way that would have staggered Mr Griffith. He would have been so excited.'

The cycle of films included two outstanding one-offs. One was *The Wind* (1928), set on the prairies of Western Texas, and unique in the Jungian resonances introduced by its intellectual Swedish director, Victor Seastrom. The shocking story starred Lillian Gish as a sheltered Virginian girl who kills the horse-dealer who has raped her and then goes mad during a dust storm after the wind uncovers his body from the sand. The score used five percussionists plus timpani, and one reviewer said that the power of the music in the storm scene had him clutching the arms of his seat in case he was blown away. Colin Matthews worked on that scene with Davis. 'Carl's own music is tonally based, and he freely admits that he is unsure of how to work in a different idiom,' says Matthews. 'The moment that anything moves out of tonality, he would turn to me. His directions for *The Wind* were purely graphic, as he wanted me to create the sound. For the storm sequence, I came up with an almost Penderecki-like sound, using high, screaming strings and five tam-tams. It created an extraordinary melange of sound, almost like an electronic score, but all done naturally.'

Colin Matthews also worked on the scoring of King Vidor's First World War film *The Big Parade*. 'I had a whole battle sequence in that,' he says. 'I had the time-code and a copy of the movie, and Carl drew me a graph within a time-slot, saying "These are the high points and the low points." I had to put the right things in the right place, and I was given precise timings, so I knew when the explosions – bass drum strokes – would happen. The storm sequence in *The Wind* had been completely free, but the battle sequence in *The Big Parade* was much more within strict tempo limits. Carl gave me blocks of musical material to use – I was taking Penderecki or early Górecki as a model. He wanted that kind of block sound. It was really challenging, and I was impressed that Carl gave me so much freedom to come up with the right sound.'

The other one-off was Erich von Stroheim's 1924 masterpiece *Greed*, set in San Francisco. 'The action was very grotesque and ugly,' says Davis, 'and I had to go much further than a film composer of the 1920s. It ended up being very dissonant, intentionally sounding like contemporary music in the classical sense of the word. In the sound-world of the 1920s, everything except possibly electronic music was already there, or was accepted by classical music audiences. But that wasn't what commercial film-making of that period was about – they wanted a broad remit. One can have a different perspective today.'

Davis says that one decision that had to be taken was whether he was going to use any pre-existing scores for silent films. He says that generally he resisted the idea, as he believed that audiences then differed from present-day audiences, in that popular classics – pieces that are taken for granted by a modern audience – would then have seemed quite fresh to a predominantly working-class audience that had little access to recorded music. But now, if you use a piece of music that is very well known, he says, it could be very distracting, as it introduces the overlay of the audience's musical experience outside the cinema. On the other hand, he says, there are existing scores that are of interest, and he felt that to resurrect those would be quite exciting. 'For a few films like D. W. Griffith's tragedy *Broken Blossoms* (1919), starring Lillian Gish, for which Louis Gottschalk wrote the original score and Griffith himself provided the sentimental "White Blossom" theme, I decided to take the original score and develop it further, make the orchestration more interesting. Films get recut and altered, and scenes get reversed. Griffith himself recut *Broken Blossoms* in the 1920s, so I had to extend certain passages to fit the variations in the cut.'

Ben-Hur

One silent film score that survives was created for the 1925 MGM version of Lew Wallace's epic novel *Ben-Hur*. The story is set in the time of Christ, and chronicles the journey of a Jewish prince through betrayal and slavery to eventual love and redemption, when Ben-Hur is converted to Christianity after witnessing Christ's crucifixion and resurrection. The 1959 remake, with an Academy Award-winning score by Miklós Rózsa, became extremely popular, but Carl Davis says that connoisseurs regard the 1925 version, shorter than the 1959 version, but still running for nearly two and a half hours, as superior. The original 1925 film contained some two-colour Technicolor sequences, as well as some that were hand-tinted, but in the prints held by MGM the Technicolor sequences had all faded to a sludge-brown and were impossible to use. (Kevin Brownlow points out that MGM insisted that that was what Technicolor looked like in the 1920s!) Brownlow eventually unearthed a fine print with all the colour sequences intact from the state archive in Prague. Meanwhile, Carl Davis had to wait until a complete version of the visual material had been assembled before he could start work on a score, in 1987.

He found a copy of the original 1925 piano score for *Ben-Hur* in the Library of Congress in Washington DC, published by MGM. 'It looks like a ballet or an opera score – it has orchestral indications and cues. I thought it had too much borrowing from Liszt, Wagner and Massenet, a real hodge-podge. I saw the film as a romantic melodrama with the New Testament story as a kind of subplot, so I decided I would treat it like a big Romantic opera, with assigned themes. Wagner (in *Lohengrin* and *Parsifal*) and Mendelssohn (in the 'Reformation' Symphony) both used a certain musical phrase, a cadence, called the Dresden Amen, which was said to have been composed by Luther. I thought that this would be interesting as the one piece of music by someone else that I could use. The key was that phrase. Everyone says I quoted Wagner, when in fact Wagner was quoting Luther. I didn't end up using any of the original score, except for the rhythm for the famous chariot race sequence, derived from *The Ride of the Valkyries.'*

David and Colin Matthews both assisted Carl with the orchestration of *Ben-Hur*. David was responsible for orchestrating the chariot race. 'It took a month, it was such a substantial feature of the film. It was *fortissimo* all the way through, and Carl wanted to use two pairs of timpani either side of the orchestra. They play all the way through the race, imitating the drumming of the horses' hooves.'

'The *Ben-Hur* score is quite a showpiece,' says Carl Davis. 'It's one of my most ambitious, using a very large orchestra. The London Philharmonic premiered it at the London Palladium, recorded it, and took it on tour. On one occasion they were booked to play at the Vienna Festival. They were given a concert in the Musikverein, and just across from there is the Wiener Konzerthaus, a very large concert hall. One night they were doing Wagner in the Musikverein and the next *Ben-Hur* in the Konzerthaus. I was amused to look at the weekly posters of events, advertising *Rienzi, Parsifal*, the St Matthew Passion, Honegger's *Jeanne d'Arc au bûcher* – and *Ben-Hur*!

The Garbo connection

The Brownlow–Gill–Davis collaboration included several films starring Greta Garbo – *Flesh and the Devil, A Woman of Affairs*, and *The Mysterious Lady*. Garbo was one of the few actors who made a successful transition from silent to talking films. While many of the silent movie actors had very strong accents, which didn't transpose to talkies, Garbo's Swedish accent wasn't overly intrusive. Audiences adored her smoky, sexy voice. When she starred in her first talkie, *Anna Christie*, in 1930, MGM advertised it with the words: 'Garbo Talks!' She had a tremendous sound-film career, especially in films of the 1930s like *Ninotchka, Grand Hotel, Anna Karenina,* and *Camille*, but in fact her first major success in America was in Clarence Brown's *Flesh and the Devil* (1926), a silent film in which she co-starred with her lover, John Gilbert.

Carl Davis says that when Garbo first came to the States, she was cast as the evil Continental lady, and *Flesh and the Devil*, which was her breakthrough film in the USA, depicted her as the villainess, but also as the victim. The suffering Garbo began to emerge in *A Woman of Affairs*, in which she became sympathetic and tragic. Davis thinks that Garbo's understated style was unique for the era, and contributed to her success. 'It looks very contemporary. When you see her perform she is surrounded in the main by people who tend to over-act, but she never does. This was a glamorous era: leading men and ladies had to have a particular look, which was largely achieved through lighting and camera angles. Garbo always looked wonderful. When I have been scoring Garbo films there always has to be a special moment, accompanied by a special string texture, for her first appearance. The world around her changes when she is there.' In *Flesh and the Devil*, Garbo delays her appearance for the first ten or so minutes, and when she does finally arrive on screen, Davis surrounds her with a voluptuous love theme, first announced on a solo violin, and then clothed in sumptuous orchestral timbres.

'We all regarded *Flesh and the Devil* as "Best Achievement",' says Colin Matthews. 'It was one score for which Carl did a first draft, and then rewrote it, because he wasn't very satisfied with the first attempt. It was a big romantic movie. We went to a screening, and sat through it without music in the first instance. I would have been completely at sea if I had had to provide 90 minutes' worth of music for it. Carl has an extraordinary knack of picking things up and running with them, and hitting exactly the right mood.'

'I was once thrilled to be conducting a live performance of that film with the Stockholm Philharmonic in their lovely, pale blue hall,' Davis recalls. 'On the other side of the square was a large department store, dating from the early 1900s, where Garbo had once worked in the millinery department. The concert hall was very full – there was a lot of curiosity about the performance, and everyone was quiet at the start. When Garbo appears for the first time, at a railway station, the place suddenly came alive – the audience were whispering as if she had appeared in person. That was a real frisson.

'The lighting, the way Garbo behaves, she invests everything with glamour, and that needs to be mirrored in the music. That thinking is part of the composition and the orchestration, you have to make it glow. The Garbo films call for original music. My score for *Flesh and the Devil* is completely original. *A Woman of Affairs* uses an exquisite Liszt piano piece, one of the Petrarch sonnets. The character she plays in my third Garbo score, *The Mysterious Lady*, is a spy, but she's also the mistress of a Russian general, and she is very glamorous. She's an opera singer, and we make repeated use of *Vissi d'arte* from *Tosca*. It starts with four and half minutes of *Tosca*, and the character continues to perform it throughout the film. As the plot thickens and she's more and more in danger of being discovered, the orchestration becomes more and more menacing and discordant – *Vissi d'arte* gets sabotaged!'

Phantom of the Opera

One of Carl Davis's all-time favourite films is *Phantom of the Opera*, based on the 1910 novel by Gaston Leroux. There have been three successive films of the novel, the first one a 1925 silent directed by Rupert Julian and starring Lon Chaney and Mary Philbin; then came the 1943 version with Claude Rains and Susanna Foster, and then the 1962 Hammer Horror remake with Herbert Lom and Heather Sears. More recently, Andrew Lloyd Webber turned it into a very successful musical. But the 1925 silent version is revered as an absolute classic.

'I always think of this film as a throwback to my early life,' says Davis, 'queuing up at the Met during a freezing New York winter to get standing room. If you got there early you could get the best spot. In the 1950s I saw Peter Brook's production of Gounod's *Faust*. That was the opera that opened the New York Met in 1883. In the 1925 film of *Phantom of the Opera*, which takes place at the Paris Opéra, there only seemed to be one opera in their repertoire, which was *Faust*. *Faust* wasn't actually premiered at the Opéra – it originally had spoken dialogue, and was put on at the Théâtre-Lyrique. Gounod later revised it, adding recitatives, extra ballets and arias. Then it was taken up by the Opéra, and became the most popular and most performed piece in the repertoire. It's very clear that the opera company in the Phantom story is performing *Faust*, and the leading lady is playing Marguérite when she is kidnapped by the Phantom. My score for the film makes full use of the opera. Is the Phantom meant to be Mephistopheles? Then I thought no, he's not the Devil, he is more multi-faceted. Almost all the film takes place in the opera house, where they are rehearsing and performing *Faust* – you see scenes which give some indication of exactly where they have got to in the opera, and I pinpoint this. But as the film progresses, I thought it would be fun to blur the reality, so that themes from the opera could find parallels with the Phantom story. I started to work with the Gounod themes and give them an extra overlay. The Phantom's story, which is my own music, runs in parallel with the Gounod. I introduced a whole new series of themes – the Phantom theme, and a Christine theme.' The scenes in the cellars and sewers under the Opéra are truly terrifying, and Davis's atmospheric score conveys a chilling atmosphere of horror. It was premiered at the 1996 Edinburgh Film Festival by the Royal Scottish National Orchestra, and a decade later, on 8 October 2006, Carl Davis conducted a live screening at the Royal Opera House, Covent Garden, in honour of his seventieth birthday.

The silent comedies: Chaplin, Lloyd, Keaton et al.

The ever-expanding catalogue of silent films restored by the Gill–Brownlow–Davis team since the late 1980s has included a substantial proportion of comedy. The three kings of comedy in the 1920s were Charlie Chaplin, Buster Keaton and Harold Lloyd. Chaplin was an unusual case. His films of the 1930s, *City Lights* and *Modern Times*, though basically silents, did have synchronised music and effects tracks, with a few words of comic dialogue. Though musically illiterate, Chaplin had a fantastic ear and a flair for melody, and he composed his own scores as well as producing, editing and starring in the films. The centenary of Chaplin's birth fell in 1989 and David Gill had the brilliant idea of performing *City Lights* live. He and Davis needed to find the original score, to compare it with the soundtrack, which Chaplin had recorded at the time.

'By the early 1920s,' says Davis, 'it was quite clear that silent films with orchestral accompaniment were on the way out. People wanted to hear dialogue and sound effects. But Chaplin must have been in crisis, worried that audiences wouldn't accept the voice of his greatest creation – the Tramp. In the end he decided that although there was some brief comedy dialogue, the Tramp would never speak, but that he himself would create and record a score. Basically he was still making silent films throughout the 1930s. After *The Great Dictator* (1940) he abandoned the Tramp character.

'Reproducing the original score of *City Lights* threw up many problems. The Chaplin archive is based in Switzerland, where Chaplin lived for the last part of his life. The scores are all kept in huge cabinets in a great underground chamber beneath a mountain in Geneva, accessed by a lift – it was like going down to Nibelheim – and there they were. I was given access to all these scores, from *City Lights* and *Modern Times* onwards. They needed a lot of work – it was all quite a mess – as I worked out how I could do *City Lights* live. It was a major reconstruction job, trying to recreate Chaplin's unique scoring. Once I had the score of *City Lights*, I took a while to work out why it differed in places from the soundtrack. I was looking at the score, and playing the sound version, and they didn't match up. Apparently, Chaplin had three weeks of recording sessions for an 86-minute film, and he reworked the score continuously. When the Chaplin office sent me a photocopy of the score, they omitted to send the extra bits that the players had pasted over the original parts during rehearsals – some of them with rude comments written over them! The glue had dried up, and they had fallen off. What I had been working from was the absolute original score, without any of the rewrites. At first, none of the people who were working with me could work out what belonged where. We had to spend hours listening to the soundtrack and trying to decipher what they were playing. The reconstruction was a painfully slow process.

'*City Lights* was premiered in 1989 with Princess Diana in attendance. It was a wonderful charity night, and I had to write a little fanfare for her – she required entrance music. David Gill practised walking between the holding area and her seat, so that we could time how long it would take. I was actually more nervous because Georg Solti was there as well!'

City Lights was a huge success, and Chaplin films with live orchestra were obviously going to be popular. But the Chaplin family was divided in their view. Chaplin had eight children by his third wife, Oona, and at that time the children were split as to whether this revival was a good idea. Apparently the ones who disagreed were talked round by the others, led by Chaplin's son Eugene, who claimed that live performances such as these would lead to a revival of interest in the films, which clearly would be of great benefit to the family.

'*The Gold Rush* and *The Kid* followed,' says Carl Davis, 'Then the composer and conductor Tim Brock did a fabulous transcription of *Modern Times* (1936), which I also took into my repertoire. During the 1980s, we made spin-offs for TV, with additional material forming new products. The first was a three-part documentary series for Thames TV called *Unknown Chaplin*, which made use of material from a recently discovered barrel of out-takes. Chaplin normally destroyed his out-takes, claiming he didn't want people to know how he worked. But because he didn't own his earliest material, made before he joined First National, there was a particular group of short films he made between 1916 and 1917 for the Mutual Film Corporation, of which he didn't own the copyright. The out-takes from these revealed that Chaplin worked from improvisation, but he printed every take, which show how he developed each scene.'

'That unknown footage was a Pandora's box of material, so much that we didn't know what to do with it all,' says Kevin Brownlow. 'These documentaries are more entertainment than factual, and I wasn't sure how to approach them, but Carl caught Chaplin's character with the simplest of themes. I thought at first it was almost too simple, and it wouldn't work, but it did, superbly.'

Davis continues: 'While working on *The Unknown Chaplin* (released in 1983), I experienced one of the most startling moments of my life. The Chaplin estate had to approve our cut. I had a working meeting scheduled with David and Kevin to go through the first episode, which dealt with Chaplin's early years, up to 1917. To my amazement Oona Chaplin and her daughter Geraldine were both sitting at the Steenbeck flatbed editing suite, watching Episode 1. I've never been in an atmosphere like it. There were Chaplin's wife and daughter watching material that they had never seen before. Oona didn't meet Charlie until 1943, when he was already a middle-aged man. Geraldine, their eldest child, was born in 1944. She would not have known her father except as an elderly man. They were looking at Charlie when he was twenty-seven – a person they did not know – and there he was, very animated, flirting with the camera. The two women were absolutely riveted by this little screen. Then I was introduced to them, and it was thrilling. Oona was very sweet and undemonstrative. Geraldine was herself a famous actress, living in Spain. She came to a performance of *City Lights* in Madrid, and to the Dutch premiere of the revived 1925 cut of *The Gold Rush*. Both of those were exciting occasions. I also had the extraordinary experience of re-opening an old theatre in Vevey with *City Lights*. Chaplin spent his final years there, in virtual exile. He had been under investigation by the FBI since the late 1940s for alleged communist sympathies, and the Americans wanted him out. He was in London for the premiere of *Limelight* in 1952, and he was warned not to try to go back to the USA. He then went to live in Switzerland, and bought a lovely house at Corsier-sur-Vevey. He and Oona had eight children, in addition to several from his previous marriages, and Geraldine told me that one of Charlie's two adult sons sent Charlie a box of condoms on the birth of each successive child.'

Brownlow and Gill had also established a good relationship with Buster Keaton's wife, Eleanor; and Harold Lloyd's grand-daughter, Suzanne, was very determined to get her grandfather's films back on the map. During the Thames TV days, Brownlow, Gill and Davis produced a series on Buster Keaton, called *A Hard Act to Follow*, and a documentary film, *The Third Genius*, on Harold Lloyd. They had already referenced several Keaton features, in particular *The General* (1927), based on a real-life incident from the American Civil War, and which includes the destruction of a full-size railway bridge and a locomotive. 'The General captures the Civil War atmosphere in a very authentic way,' says Kevin Brownlow. 'Why Keaton chose to make a comedy so authentic is extraordinary, but Carl reflected that atmosphere in his use of original music from the time.'

The list of Keaton films also includes *Our Hospitality*, a comedy-thriller involving some spectacular stunts, and the classic short *One Week*, in which Keaton tries to assemble a D.I.Y. house he has been given for a wedding present. Davis says that the Rohauer Collection of Keaton films is now in the hands of building magnate Charles Cohen. He has ambitious plans for the catalogue, which includes most of Keaton's features and shorts. Davis has also scored another Keaton feature, *Steamboat Bill Jr*, with two more Keaton shorts on the agenda.

The Davis catalogue also includes several major Lloyd comedies – *The Kid Brother, Safety Last* (which includes the classic 'human fly' stunt on a skyscraper), and *Speedy* (set in evocative New York locations), all of which have accompanying scores inspired by the popular jazz band music of the 1920s. These have been reissued by an American DVD firm called Criterion. Davis has also scored *The Freshman* and *Why Worry?*, both of which have been performed in Europe and the USA. After a Los Angeles premiere, Suzanne Lloyd wrote a touching letter to Carl Davis, saying how grateful she was: 'You have given me the gift of magic for my grandfather's films.'

Chaplin's *Mutuals*

The Thames TV connection began to dissolve in the early 1990s after Thames lost its broadcasting franchise in 1992. Sold to Fremantle, it remains a production house. At that point Channel 4 started to commission the films directly, while Thames helped David and Kevin to form a production company of their own, Photoplay. During the 1980s they were turning out up to three films a year, but it gradually dwindled to one a year, and not all the scores were by Davis. Then in 2000, Channel 4, which had taken over the finance for the silent presentations, decided to cut the cord.

'At that point,' says Davis, 'I thought here we had this unique repertoire, recognised as a genuine genre in its own right. I thought there must be some way in which I can have a controlling interest in this material. So far as Chaplin films are concerned, the Chaplin estate had always existed as a going concern. Chaplin had kept all his copyrights. We don't own the scores. But there is a large amount of pre-1917 public domain material including the extraordinary *Mutuals* – the twelve shorts he'd made in 1916 and 1917 for the Mutual Production Company. He was very well paid for them. He formed a company to act in them, consisting of all the necessary actors, including the pretty girl, the heavy, an older woman, and various types of comic male characters. When Chaplin talked about the *Mutuals*, he said it was the happiest time of his life when he was working on them.

'The project seemed very promising for us. The problem was finding good-quality prints. I knew the collector David Shepard, who had access to good prints. He was totally committed to silent films, and he was completely supportive. He thought it was a great idea. My publisher Faber Music struck a deal for the prints, and I would compose scores for these twelve short films. Many had some autobiographical content – one is called *The Immigrant*, about two people meeting and falling in love on an immigrant steamer bound for America. In *Easy Street* Chaplin plays a tramp who is drawn to a street mission, vows to reform in order to win the love of a young woman, and becomes a policeman; in *The Fireman* he rescues a young woman from a burning house. I devised a lecture, and pointed out that if you choose clips from them, you can see the story of Chaplin's life up to that point emerging. It's fascinating.

'When Chaplin was at the height of his fame in the 1930s he became friends with Nancy Astor, who lived then at Cliveden. I was asked to give this lecture at Cliveden. It's a huge villa-like house, with an amazingly grand approach, a massive fountain and a lovely park. As I was giving the lecture in one of the reception rooms, I was thinking about Chaplin, who spent part of his childhood in a Lambeth workhouse and reached the depths of deprivation. What could he have been thinking as he swept up the drive of that house? That was a big journey.

'I undertook the *Mutuals* in around 2000. The series has proved to be my best-seller. You can use one of them as a curtain-raiser to a full-length feature, and perhaps I could relate the choice of short to the feature. Or you could programme three shorts in one evening, or all twelve across a weekend.

'When I started working on the *Mutuals*, I realised that there is a very specific technique involved in scoring comedy. Back in 1989 I studied Charlie's own scores for his sound films very carefully – when should the music take over, when should you step back, how much should you illustrate – because to some extent the comedy in silent films was taken over by animated cartoons. Cartoons can make a reality of what is impossible, but the origin of this technique lies in silent film comedy. The Disney cartoons evolved a special kind of scoring in which every little gesture, every act, is mimicked musically. You could look at silent films from that point of view, but if you look carefully at Chaplin's own scores, from the 1930s on, especially *City Lights* and *Modern Times*, there are places where he doesn't mimic. Mostly he conceives his scores in whole paragraphs devoted to a specific character.

'Each of the great comics has an individual personality, and you have to understand what brings them to life, what's their aura. You also have to think of their objective, what is it that they are trying to do. Lloyd and Keaton always set themselves a problem – I've got to capture my locomotive, I've got to make more money, I've got to hide something from being seen. They always have an objective, and the score's function is to help them achieve their aim. Whether it's stopping a train, or climbing a skyscraper, you have to be there with them. Even in Chaplin films where there is an obvious sound-effect, he sometimes ignores it, knowing that the audience is going to understand. You must tread a fine line between mimicking, and providing a sustained piece of music, within which the incidents fall as if predictable. You have to convey the feel of any particular scene or action. For me, working on these Chaplin scores was an education.'

Over the past thirty-five years, the partnership of Carl Davis, Kevin Brownlow and David Gill (who tragically died in 1997, and whose role in the company was taken over by Patrick Stanbury) has created a whole new genre, Live Cinema, and revealed the splendours of a film repertoire that had seemed lost for ever. To cope with the sheer volume of these silent film commissions, Davis had to search for further gifted orchestrators and he mentions two in particular. David Cullen, who was Andrew Lloyd Webber's frequent choice (for *Cats* and *Phantom*), orchestrated the jazz sequences of *The Crowd* brilliantly and helped stitch together Rimsky-Korsakov for *The Thief of Bagdad*. He also worked on *Show People*, the film *Champions* and the ballet *A Simple Man*. Nic Raine, who had worked with John Barry on several Bond scores, was Davis's principal copyist on *Napoléon* – a heroic task which earned Carl's eternal gratitude – and went on to orchestrate *Phantom*, *The General* and *Safety Last*.

As Davis says, other people have now followed in his footsteps, making careers out of creating, recording and performing music for silent films. 'Other conductors have wanted to take it up, and so the scores had to be made available – which has been done through my publisher, Faber Music. A new breed of conductors who perform silent film scores has sprung up. Each evolves an individual method of how to do it, but we help them as much as we can, working on how you rehearse it. I think about how I can help other conductors to synchronise and perform the film.'

Many Live Cinema events take place at international film festivals. 'These huge film festivals are like shopping malls,' says Davis. 'People come from all over to see what may be available. One of the most successful is the autumn festival in the Italian city of Pordenone, just outside Venice. We've had great success there since 1987 when we performed *The Wind*. That festival is a solid week of 24/7 silent film showings – you get pianists carried out on stretchers! – and they usually close the festival with a live orchestral score. Another important venue is Luxembourg, where the films are presented by the enterprising Cinémathèque Lux. I have performed there every year since 1987.'

'There have been other attempts to score for silent movies, following on in the tradition of the Thames Silents,' says Colin Matthews, 'but no one ever thought of it before Carl started. I've heard other scores, but they don't enter into the spirit of the movie enough, they try to be too sophisticated. The world of the silent movie is not very sophisticated. It allows you a lot of imagination, but the films are really quite simple, with big emotions, and you can't convey those by having a score that is over-sophisticated. Carl's scores tap into exactly the right mood – he hits the nail on the head. Some people say that they vulgarise them, but that's what the films were like. Carl's music is so much better than the fragments of original music from that period that survive.'

The film composer and pianist Neil Brand agrees. 'Carl paved the way for all of us – his work on *Napoléon*, the Thames silents, the Hollywood TV series and the many Channel 4 silents set the bar higher than anybody since (and possibly including) the silent period.'

V

ON CONDUCTING

When Carl Davis raised his baton for the premiere of *Napoléon* at the Empire Theatre on 30 November 1980, he was making his first major public appearance as a conductor. When he came to England in 1960, the idea of performing was not uppermost in his mind. For the past twenty years he had been working primarily as a composer, and occasionally as a musical director, but he had never thought of himself as a conductor, other than in the studio. From that moment onwards, conducting would play a major role in his future career.

It was not, of course, the first time he had stood in front of an orchestra. 'During my teenage years, as soon as I began to compose and record, I had started to conduct in college. At the same time I was absorbing music, coaching people in their roles at New York City Opera and the Robert Shaw Chorale. I learned a great deal from those years when I was playing and assisting. I had been given informal conducting lessons from helpful conductors during the time when I was working with opera workshops, Gilbert & Sullivan societies, and so on. There were people who were helping me out and giving me tips. But I have never been to a formal conducting class. I can see now that it would have been helpful. My conducting approach mostly developed through the 1960s to the 1980s, when I did an enormous amount of studio work, but that didn't involve standing up in front of an audience. In a studio situation, I'm king. We have three hours, and most of the time what we do in those hours must please me, but also has to please other people as well. In film music, you have to be very professional, very skilled, technically and musically, and you have to have an instinct as to what will work on film.

'Then from 1980 onwards I had to start to think of myself as a conductor, which had never been in my mindset. There was one warm-up event, a concert in June 1980 at the Fairfield Halls in Croydon at which I conducted the Wren Orchestra of London in the premiere of my own First Symphony, which had been commissioned by Capital Radio. That was in a way my first concert. Then, on 30 November 1980, I found myself conducting – in public – a five-hour score that had to be precisely synchronised to fit an extremely long film. I had so much to think about, quite apart from my own physical survival and the stamina required by the orchestra to play at such Wagnerian lengths. I had already had a great deal of experience in a studio environment, working with time-codes and click-tracks. But I had never done it live before. You can't stop and correct and do a retake. That was an extraordinary day. I got through it with a mixture of bravery, helpful ignorance, a great deal of luck and a co-operative orchestra. We had one major setback, in the middle of Act Three, when owing to the sheer weight of musical material on some of the stands, the music fell off, and things broke down. A very private recording exists in which I am screaming "Play! Play!" while the players scrabble around on the floor trying to pick up their music.

'Having re-invented the concept of performing silent film scores with a live orchestra from fleapit to the Royal Festival Hall, I found myself living a double existence as composer and conductor. These are separate skills, but they came together for me in the silent films.

'I never had a vision of the conductor as fantasy figure. Conducting for me is a form of communication. The conductor's job is to provide the impetus, and make clear what is going on in the score. There is a code: the music has a shape, whether it's simple, or complex, or even in some contemporary music, free. You are an organiser from every point of view; you must convey what is to be played and its meaning. It's an art you learn as you go along. After conducting for a very long time, I'm still learning how to do it, and

I'm still surprised if I'm complimented on it. I'm just doing what I do. What's interesting is the relationship with the orchestra.

'My conducting career grew out of my adaptation of the old silent film practice of using some classical repertoire as film music. In the days when people had limited access to gramophone records and live music, the use of classical music in the cinema had an educative function. People began to hear some of these pieces for the first time, which are now so well known. I feel that that still holds true today. When I recently went to see the film *The King's Speech*, I was astonished at the climactic moment to discover that the backing track was the slow movement from Beethoven's Seventh Symphony, which I had incorporated in my *Napoléon* score. Beethoven's music is a central theme in that score, together with symphonies by Haydn and Mozart. I found they helped to set the story and gave it a corset.'

Working with the Philharmonia

Davis's use of classical excerpts in his silent film scores provided him with an entrée into the conducting world. One of the players in the Wren Orchestra at the screening of *Napoléon* was the bass player Gerald Drucker, who was also principal bass at the Philharmonia. Gerald ran the London Double Bass Quartet, who had played Davis's score for Mike Leigh's 1982 TV film *Home Sweet Home*, and it was Drucker who suggested to the Philharmonia that they might engage Davis as a conductor for live concerts. His first date with the orchestra was on 15 January 1983, at the Fairfield Halls in Croydon, and Davis was only allowed a single rehearsal for an ambitious programme. It consisted of music associated with well-known feature films – the opening of Richard Strauss's *Also sprach Zarathustra* and Johann Strauss's *Blue Danube* Waltz (from Stanley Kubrick's *2001: A Space Odyssey*), Mussorgsky's *Night on the Bare Mountain* and Dukas's *The Sorcerer's Apprentice* (from Disney's *Fantasia*), the *Adagietto* from Mahler's Fifth Symphony (used very effectively in Visconti's *Death in Venice*), the third movement from Brahms's Third Symphony (used in *Goodbye Again*, the 1961 film adaptation of a novel by Françoise Sagan), and Bernstein's *Symphonic Dances from 'West Side Story'*. It ended with Ravel's *Bolero*, which had been used to great effect in *10*, starring Dudley Moore and Bo Derek, as the top piece (in the order of one to ten) that people would choose to make love to. 'That programme was an interesting challenge,' says Davis. 'It needed intensive preparation. I was dealing with a major orchestra, and each major orchestra has an individual character. It went off respectably, and we repeated it at the Barbican the following night.

'Then word got round, and I started to build a parallel career as a conductor. I realised that if I was to run a career as a conductor and composer, I needed an agent and a manager, so I teamed up with Paul Wing, who had previously managed the English Chamber Orchestra. He worked with me for twenty-three years, and oversaw the evolution of my conducting career, as well as the technical performances of the silent films.'

Carl Davis may not have invented the concept of themed concerts of classical pops, but he did a great deal to popularise it in the UK. 'I thought it would be fascinating to explore a theme in some depth. For instance, an evening on the theme of the American West could show the story of the development of the USA itself – the move from the east to the west coasts. It can be expressed not only through film music, but also theatre music and dance. Many symphonic pieces have been inspired by the story of the USA.' Other orchestras saw that Carl's concerts with the Philharmonia were proving extremely popular, and before long he got an offer to conduct the Bournemouth Symphony for ten themed concerts a year, between 1984 and 1987. He was offered a similar three-year deal with the London Philharmonic, and other contracts followed with the Hallé and the Royal Liverpool Philharmonic.

The Liverpool connection

Carl's long association with Liverpool and its orchestra started in the 1980s, when his wife Jean was playing Mrs Boswell in *Bread*, and Carl became involved in an interesting collaboration with

Bread's writer Carla Lane (who sadly passed away in 2016). They created three stories about animals for narrator and orchestra, in the style of *Peter and the Wolf.* He then devised an orchestral evening celebrating the city of Liverpool. 'Liverpool is not only the story of the Beatles, but also of the rise of the whole British pop scene. It also has many extremely gifted poets and writers. I brought in Roger McGough, and the playwright Willy Russell, who had had great success with his play *Educating Rita* and the musical *Blood Brothers.*' Then came *Paul McCartney's Liverpool Oratorio* in 1991, followed two years later by the establishment of the Liverpool Summer Pops.

'The CEO of the Royal Liverpool Philharmonic was a Canadian ex-horn player called Robert Creech. He knew about the Boston Symphony's long and highly successful series of Boston Pops concerts. In the early 1990s the concert hall in Liverpool, which was then owned by the orchestra, was a terrible mess. It was crumbling, and was about to be closed for a long period. There was no other suitable hall in which to perform. Robert had the idea of hiring a Big Top and pitching it on the banks of the Mersey, on King's Dock between the Beatles Museum and the VAT office. A more windswept setting couldn't be imagined! He suggested we should put on a season in the Big Top, so we planned a summer series of eight concerts, over two or three weeks. I wanted to use the Boston pattern – of three short "acts" of around twenty-five minutes each. One of the great attractions of the Boston Pops was that they cleared the stalls of seats, and brought in tiny tables and chairs, like a café. People could buy refreshments during the concert. As well as adopting the tables, we installed the longest bar in Europe.

'We put on an American Night, a Viennese Night, a Western Night, and a Last Night of the Pops – for which the programme was even lighter than for the Last Night of Proms, but nevertheless ended in similar patriotic mode. There were afternoon concerts for children, and the first year we screened Buster Keaton's *The General.* We also had Bond nights narrated by Honor Blackman with excerpts from the James Bond film scores; a Spanish night with Paco Peña's flamenco troupe, and so on. People loved these concerts.

'The Summer Pops season gave me the opportunity to confront the whole ethic of performing. I remember someone from Capital Radio remarking about the audience at a classical concert: "Everyone's so still!" Traditionally, at a classical concert, the audience is passive, receiving the music, but not in a physical way. I could see there was a problem concerning the world of classical music. Where is it? What is it about? It seems in some way to belong to the sphere of church, school, even army; it seemed a punitive experience. How should you dress? How should you behave? These are not things you know instinctively. Not everyone has the privilege of early entry into what seems to be a private, exclusive world. People wouldn't know how to behave unless they had been taken to concerts. I wanted my concerts to be different, to be fun. There was a bar, there was a restaurant, there were impromptu jazz performances before and afterwards. People from the orchestra told me that they were seeing faces in the Big Top that they never saw at concerts in the hall. We started off with audiences of two thousand, and ended with over four thousand. The concerts became a major fixture of the summer season. It just got better and better.'

Davis says he was concerned about the look of the orchestra – should the conductor be wearing formal dress, or not? He addressed the problem in a manner consistent with his impish sense of humour. 'My opening concert was a Viennese Night with many encores. I had programmed the Eduard Strauss railway polka *Bahn frei*, which has sound effects – train whistles and so on – written into the score. The stage manager told me that the backstage crew had a bet going that I wouldn't wear a British Rail cap to conduct it. I thought, "OK, it's a dare." I put the cap on and walked out. Jaws dropped, and then the place exploded in laughter and cheers! It seemed so startling: there was an immaculately dressed conductor in a tail-coat suddenly walking on stage wearing a railwayman's cap. I thought that there was definitely value in this. It seemed to have made such a deep impression. So I decided that dressing up could become a permanent feature in these concerts. I established a style, and the audience laughed, or applauded, or were astonished.

I encouraged them to react. I began to have fun, dressing up in all sorts of appropriate costumes. For Western Night I came on in jeans and a fringed jacket. I even came on in a Pink Panther costume! (His wife Jean recalls trying to squeeze him into it.) Then I invited the orchestra to dress up. I once did a "Relaxed" concert, and asked the orchestra to dress as if they were chilling out. They couldn't all come in pyjamas, so I asked them to think about what they did to relax. We ended up with the two girls on the front desk of violins playing the slow movement of the Bach Double Concerto dressed in long, flowing robes and barefoot, while behind them the piccolo player was giving yoga lessons, and the principal flute was giving golf tips. A lot of the players came in motorcycle gear, and some in riding kit. There was an amazingly relaxed feeling about the playing, too. They were all amusing each other. Sometimes, it did get rather out of hand, when the orchestra turned up for a Halloween concert looking like ghouls. They would never tell me what they were going to do, which was all part of the fun.'

Davis's association with Liverpool has been recognised by the award of two honorary degrees from Liverpool's universities – an Honorary Fellowship from Liverpool John Moores University in 1992, and in 2002 an Honorary D. Mus. from Liverpool University in recognition of his work with the RLPO.

The great outdoors

Since the 1980s, Davis has also conducted concerts outdoors during the summer, starting with the Philharmonia's annual *al fresco* concert at Leeds Castle in Kent. 'Leeds Castle has a spectacular setting. It's a gorgeous stately home surrounded by a moat, beautifully maintained. They hosted international conferences there. In 1984, Christopher Bishop, then the chief executive of the Philharmonia, thought that I would be a good person to conduct the summer concerts at Leeds Castle. I conducted them consistently for twenty-four years. Unfortunately the events organisers at the castle didn't seem to get the idea that they needed a firm contract with the orchestra for specific dates, and gradually the

Philharmonia started to be booked elsewhere. From 1989 the Royal Philharmonic Orchestra took over, and the same thing happened with them, and then for four years they imported the Luxembourg Radio Orchestra, with which I had worked on and off since 1987 on silent films. We had to communicate only in French, and they created panic at the Passport Office, as the musicians weren't just from Luxembourg; they came from all over the world!

'The concerts traditionally ended with Tchaikovsky's *1812 Overture*, complete with chorus and organ, tubular bells, cannon – and fireworks. In the early years, there was no protective covering for the orchestra. It took several years to convince the organisers to provide a covered stage. One year, it was especially cold and windy. The orchestra was placed towards the bottom of a steep, grassy slope. First of all, one of the percussionists came hurtling down the slope, shouting desperately: "Monsieur! Monsieur! Les cloches sont tombés!" And indeed, the wind had blown the tubular bell frame over, and the bells were slowly rolling down the slope towards the moat. Then, during the performance, the wind changed direction, and when the fireworks were set off, they were blown towards the players. I couldn't see anything, as I was enveloped in smoke. The orchestra had disappeared, and all you could smell was gunpowder, mixed in with the unmistakable odours of kebab and hamburger, drifting down from the fast food stalls at the top of the hill. The fireworks invaded the percussion section. Some of the women players had their hair singed, and there were great holes in the timpani, which had been hired from the LPO!

'The next year, the Luxembourg orchestra was re-engaged. The timpanist was an exuberant Californian lady called Bonnie, and she approached the orchestra manager carrying a white hard hat, such as builders wear on site. Bonnie announced that the ladies of the percussion section were taking no chances and intended to wear those during the *1812 Overture*. "Impossible!" said the manager, a Belgian noted for his fiery temper. Nevertheless, just as we began the hushed chords of the opening of the overture, the ladies of the percussion section produced their protective helmets and placed them reverently on their heads, with great delicacy. That night, the wind didn't change!

'The Leeds Castle annual open-air concert became so popular, with audiences of over thirty thousand people, that one year there was a five-mile traffic jam, and Kent Council asked us to put on more than one event. After four years of using the Luxembourg orchestra, it became too expensive as they had to be housed, and although I urged the organisers to use another London orchestra, who would not need overnights, the Royal Liverpool Philharmonic was engaged. While they were down in the south of England, I also conducted some concerts of popular programmes with them in Woking Football Stadium, but after three consecutive wet summers, the idea was dropped. There are serious physical obstacles to overcome when staging outdoor events in England – principally the weather. Musicians have to find some very inventive ways of defying the wind and holding their music on the stands. But audiences seem to love the outdoors aspect, and on a still, warm evening the effect can be magical. Such evenings are quite rare, unfortunately. I remember conducting an outdoor concert at Hatfield House – an "Old World, New World" concert with Dvořák's "New World" Symphony and Gershwin's *Rhapsody in Blue*. It was pouring with rain and I said to my manager Paul that surely no one would come. "You'll be surprised," he replied. And indeed, there appeared a procession of ghosts – hundreds of people in white plastic macs. I had a spectral audience. The applause was admittedly weak, perhaps because they all were holding umbrellas. It was the sound of one hand clapping. I should have told them to wave their umbrellas!'

Comic encounters

Over the years, in addition to his popular themed concerts, Carl Davis has worked with comedians in the context of orchestral evenings. It started when he was working with the Bournemouth Symphony, when he first worked with Steve Nallon, the voice of Mrs Thatcher on *Spitting Image*, the break-through TV political satire series using puppets. Nallon had developed a comedy act based on his Thatcher impersonation. At the same time, Davis devised a show with the satirical writer and actor John Wells, with whom he had collaborated on several television projects, as well as the musical *The Projector* for Joan Littlewood's Theatre Workshop. Wells had been responsible for *Anyone for Denis?* (a stage adaptation of the 'Dear Bill' series of satirical letters in *Private Eye*), in which he played Denis Thatcher. Davis and Wells developed the concept that Thatcher, not wanting to be upstaged by Ted Heath in the cultural arena, would send Denis out to 'do culture'. The show was initially performed by the English Chamber Orchestra at the Brighton Pavilion, on the eve of the final day of the 1984 Tory Party Conference. That was the day on which the IRA blew up the Grand Hotel, and narrowly missed killing the Prime Minister. 'I learned that day that there are certain events which cannot be upstaged,' says Davis.

He subsequently worked with Billy Connolly on a reading of William McGonagall's truly terrible poem on the 1879 Tay Bridge Disaster, which they presented as a grand Victorian melodrama. Davis and Connolly eventually developed the idea into a themed Scottish evening called *Scotland: The Truth*, accompanied by the London Symphony Orchestra. Another collaboration, on operatic selections, was with the comedy duo Hinge and Bracket, telling the story of the rise and fall of the 'Rosa Charles Opera Company'. The most ambitious of these comic encounters, however, was a grand evening called *The Last Night of the Poms*, which Davis devised in 1981 with the Australian comedian Barry Humphries. The show starred Humphries' two *alter egos*, Sir Les Patterson, Cultural Attaché to the Court of St James, and Dame Edna Everage, Housewife Megastar. Davis was to be their maestro. 'It was a delight collaborating with Barry. He has a great gift for song-writing. We did an Overture on Australian Themes, a Prokofiev take-off with narrator called 'Peter and the Shark', and a grand cantata for chorus and soloists, called *The Song of Australia*, which was a potted history of the continent from Dame Edna's viewpoint. This was my boldest take on comedy. The premiere was in the highly appropriate setting of the Royal Albert Hall. It was a great foil for Barry. LWT filmed and broadcast it, and we made an LP. Two years later we performed it on a six-week Australian tour, in Sydney and Melbourne. Barry was so brilliant, he could fire off gags like bullets. The evening ended with showers of gladioli, flung from the stage. I even conducted with one!

'Working with Barry was an extraordinary experience. It really opened me out as a performer. There was something magical about the interchange and trust between Barry and his public. The more he baited them, the more they adored him. They loved to be near him, in the front row, eager to be chosen to be tortured. We revived *The Last Night of the Poms* at the Royal Albert Hall in 2009, twenty-eight years after we conceived it.' Humphries, as Dame Edna, paid tribute to his co-conspirator, describing him as 'the only musical genius who has ever upstaged me, long may his baton twitch!'

As well as high points in Davis's long career as a conductor, there have been occasional lows. One of these was a concert in Australia, when he produced a performance of Walton's *Façade* with the Sitwell poems recited by a former Australian Prime Minister and his wife. 'The only line they got right was "Flo the kangaroo",' says Davis. On another occasion, he was conducting a *Faschingskonzert* in Munich and thought – rather cruelly – that it would be amusing to allow the gentlemen of the chorus to sing *There is Nothing Like a Dame* from *South Pacific* with German, rather than American, accents. 'We tried to get them American sailor hats, but there were none available. Someone had a contact at the film studio where *Das Boot* had been made, and the chorus ended up wearing U-boat sailor hats, not seen in Munich since 1945. There was a stunned silence when they came on, then a huge round of applause. It was like something out of *The Producers*!

'But topping the list in absurdity was a water-themed concert with the Wren Orchestra, for the Henley Festival. The Festival followed hard on the heels of the Henley Regatta, and the director had the ambitious idea of placing the orchestra on a floating stand in the middle of the Thames, flanked by fountains. Part One, which took place in daylight, went well. But after sunset the tide began to rise, and the fountains slowly disappeared beneath the water. Only their submerged lights continued to glow dimly, like the lights on the *Titanic*. Then, as dusk fell, the brilliant floodlights attracted a swarm of biting insects. The players desperately tried to swat them away: the woodwind and brass section swallowed mouthfuls of bugs with every breath. On the front desk of violins, the distinguished second violinist of the Gabrieli Quartet held out his instrument to me, complaining indignantly: "This violin is a Stradivarius, and its F holes are full of greenfly!" Ever afterwards, I habitually referred to the Festival's director as "Lord of the Flies"!

'When you are conducting, you are engaged in a technical process. In a concert situation, you are working on three levels. You must focus on the music, and its effect on the audience. The third level is the orchestra itself. You are working with a group of highly committed people, and you have to communicate with them. I feel I'm now much better at establishing a rapport with a group of musicians, and understanding them. As a conductor, you're in a social situation with a number of highly talented individuals who have to be given a common purpose. That must be communicated almost entirely physically. You can't talk your way through it – it's all about how you move, and if you are able to convey an understanding of the music through movement. It's a kind of choreography, and I find it more and more fascinating.'

VI

MUSIC FOR FEATURE FILMS

In tandem with his scores for silent movies, Carl Davis has provided music for many feature films. In this, he joins a distinguished roster of composers who have written music for film soundtracks, ranging from those for whom such music has been a useful sideline, such as Walton, Vaughan Williams, Prokofiev, Shostakovich and Copland – to those who have built very successful careers primarily as film composers, such as Erich Korngold, Miklós Rózsa, Bernard Herrmann and John Williams.

One of the secrets of Carl Davis's success is that he treats all the varied aspects of his work with absolute equality, and with a refreshing lack of pretentiousness. He has great respect for the craftsmanlike element of the work of great composers of the past, such as Haydn, Mozart and Beethoven. 'I find it fascinating to remember that all these guys had actual jobs. There was no PRS then; they had to sell their music outright, which accounts for the huge quantities of music they wrote. Mozart wrote a set of minuets right at the end of his life – he was still writing music for quite trivial commissions. At that time you sold your music to whoever would buy it. They relied on it for their income, and they had to keep producing it. There was no resting on royalties. They had to take even menial commissions seriously. They wrote for the theatre, they wrote dance music, music for the church, for military bands, music to eat to. Through their music, you always sense their craftsmanship and their personalities.'

This respect for craftsmanship has underpinned Davis's own work in different fields. 'Not long after I had arrived in the UK in the early 1960s, a British composer once told me that he had two *personae* – one when he wrote for film, and another when he wrote concert works, and that the two styles were totally different. I responded that I took the opposite approach. I was always the same person, even when I was working in diverse fields. I just responded to the project. My style was going to come through, always identifiable. I don't become another composer when I'm working in different genres – I stay the same.'

Davis has been providing music for feature films for half a century. His work in this field pre-dates his silent-film scores, but has been less regular. 'When you're handed a silent film you've got to make the sound. You must bring out the element of conversation, or the meaning of it, at least. If, after a performance of one of the silent films, someone says to me: "I was so engrossed that I didn't notice the music at all", I know that the music has actually drawn them in. With contemporary films, the score is the third element, because you have dialogue, sound effects, and then the score. Sometimes it's more effective not to have music at all. It's not *the* most important sound, it's one of the important sounds.'

Early feature films

During the 1960s Davis began to work on TV projects with the director Jack Gold, who asked him to write the music for his first feature film, *The Bofors Gun* (1968). The film, which was set in Germany just after World War II, was developed from a stage play by John McGrath and had a formidable cast of actors led by Nicol Williamson, David Warner, Ian Holm and John Thaw. The Second World War also provided the backdrop for Davis's next feature film score, Bent Christensen's *The Only Way* (1970), starring Jane Seymour as a Jewish ballet teacher in occupied Denmark during the war. He found the subject a fascinating one. 'The subject of *The Only Way* was how the Danish people saved their Jews. It was a unique story. There is a place in Denmark where there is the tiniest little channel between Denmark and Sweden, opposite Elsinore, it's the narrowest point. A fleet of fishing boats managed to ferry the bulk of Denmark's Jews to safety in Sweden. A friend of mine whom I met when I was living in Denmark was saved in that way as a baby, with his nanny and his brother. *The Only Way* was one of the first films to deal with that subject.'

Davis's television connections, particularly his work on satirical programmes such as *That Was The Week That Was* with Ned Sherrin, provided the impetus for his next commission, the soundtrack for *Up Pompeii* (1971). 'It was an adaptation of a Plautus comedy, which had been turned into a successful musical (*A Funny Thing Happened on the Way to the Forum*) with a score by Stephen Sondheim, and then into a successful TV sitcom starring Frankie Howerd as the knowing servant in a rather chaotic household. It was produced by Ned Sherrin, who devised three Frankie Howerd films on the "Up" theme. I did two of them. The first one sold very well.'

The French Lieutenant's Woman

A decade later, Davis secured his first big break as a composer for feature films, when he was brought in to work on the score of Karel Reisz's *The French Lieutenant's Woman*. 'In the first instance they wanted me to do an editing job for them. They had used a lot of music as a temp track, and they wanted to keep a lot of it. So the job started as something very disappointing. They wanted to use big chunks of Schoenberg's *Verklärte Nacht*. I just saw the first couple of reels, with this Schoenberg music, and I happened to know that the Schoenberg Estate was very protective of the composer's music. They didn't like people using it in other media, or altering it in any way. I thought to myself, "I'm going to wait a bit and see what happens." The producer, Leon Clore, asked me if there was any way of dissuading his director from using this music, as the Schoenberg Estate's financial demands were exorbitant. When I saw them the next day, I had with me a cassette of my music for *Our Mutual Friend*, which was actually a sextet (like the scoring of *Verklärte Nacht*). It was also inspired by that late romantic idiom. I wasn't being devious, but I did behave politically. I knew the story, but it wasn't for me to resolve the crisis – they had to make a decision.

'I worked very closely with Karel on the score of *The French Lieutenant's Woman*. It was an engrossing and emotionally exhausting experience. The atmosphere was very febrile. Establishing the right mood from the start of the film proved very difficult. When I began, I went through my usual routine, I would play it to them on the piano, accompanied by images on the screen, a TV monitor propped up on top of my piano. I played what I had written, which was very stormy. Karel considered it. "This piece suggests that something tragic is going to happen. But it doesn't." I offered to come back with something different. A few days later Karel returned to hear my second version. After a pause, he said, "But it sounds rather sad! And it's not sad!" So I said: "I've had two goes, and the message seems to be wrong. Tell me what you think the audience should know. A woman dressed in a long, black, hooded cape is walking along a long sea-wall with waves crashing on either side of her, and stops, staring out to sea. What should the music be telling us?" Karel replied: "This is very difficult. I think what we want to convey is the feeling that she is longing for life, for love, for experience. The music has to convey a sense of longing." I told him to go away and come back tomorrow, and then I wrote the theme music in ten minutes. These things are never literal. You have to get inside the mind of the central character, which is why they liked the Schoenberg so much.'

The title music Carl came up with, known as 'Sarah's Theme', has proved to be one of the most iconic themes in late twentieth-century film music – a haunting viola solo, its fragmented phrases the essence of passionate longing, played over a turbulent background of tremolo strings, conjuring up both mental turmoil and the presence of the unquiet sea. The velvety texture, restricted to strings and harps, evokes the late Romantic world of *Verklärte Nacht,* Schoenberg's instrumental response to a poem about love, yearning and betrayal – themes that are explored in *The French Lieutenant's Woman*. Davis's score went on in 1982 to win a BAFTA for Best Film Music, beating a particularly strong field which included Vangelis's score for *Chariots of Fire* and John Williams's for *Raiders of the Lost Ark*, and was nominated for a GRAMMY award. The theme tune also won an Ivor Novello award in the same year.

Not every project ends happily. While Davis was working on *The French Lieutenant's Woman*, he also was invited to write the score for Fred Zinnemann's last film – *Five Days One Summer*, which is set in the Alps, and has the same story as Henze's opera *Elegy for Young Lovers*. David Matthews worked with Davis on that project. 'We created very elaborate pastiches of Bruckner,' says Matthews. 'We thought it was all going well, that Zinnemann was happy with it. We recorded the whole score, and then Zinnemann said, "No, I don't think so." He thought it was too upfront. He wanted something that people wouldn't notice. I have found in my own experience that film directors often don't know what they want until they hear it.' Carl Davis says that at one point Zinnemann rounded on him, saying: 'The problem with your music is that everyone wants to listen to it!' The score was replaced, and the film wasn't a success.

'There is no film composer who has not had scores "pulled". It comes with the package. Walton's music for Guy Hamilton's epic *Battle of Britain* was rejected, except for one section, "Battle in the Air", which was kept in at Laurence Olivier's insistence – he threatened to remove his name from the credits otherwise. They replaced Walton's score with one by Ron Goodwin. I'm proud to say that I was largely responsible for resurrecting Walton's original music and performing it in concert. I read about it – what a scandal it was – and I got to know Lady Walton. We premiered it at the Colston Hall in Bristol, performed by the Bournemouth Symphony Orchestra.'

Champions

In 1983 Davis provided the score for *Champions*, directed by his old friend and neighbour John Irvin. *Champions* told the true story of the jockey Bob Champion (played by John Hurt) who was fighting testicular cancer, and the racehorse Aldaniti, who had suffered a career-threatening injury to his leg, and was in danger of being put down. Both of them seemed finished, and the film told the story of their clawback to triumph, when they won the 1981 Grand National. '*Champions* contained some very exciting footage,' says Carl Davis. 'John described it as a quest, a crusade, the determination to win. I composed and recorded the title theme without seeing any pictures – they said they would fit the footage to my music, which was a great compliment. The same thing happened with the Grand National sequence. I'm now woven into sport legend, because for years, when they staged the actual Grand National, they played the *Champions* theme, and the jockeys wept.' The opening title-sequence of the film has passed into legend. A single racehorse in training gallops against a misty skyline to the accompaniment of a distant horn solo, which then, as the camera pans on to the fences of a racecourse, swells into a triumphant theme on full orchestra bolstered by a piano. (The inclusion of piano timbre in his film scores is one of the characteristic hallmarks of Davis's orchestration, derived from the ubiquitous piano found in silent film scores.) Both Elaine Paige and Shirley Bassey have recorded 'Sometimes', a song created from the *Champions* theme music. 'And they charted!' crows Davis.

King David

Davis's next foray into feature films was less successful, but interesting in a different way. In 1985 he was invited to compose a score for *King David*, a period version of the biblical story directed by the distinguished Australian director Bruce Beresford. It starred Richard Gere, the major Hollywood actor who had just done *American Gigolo* and *An Officer and a Gentleman,* and later went on to do *Pretty Woman*. *King David* was the last major movie on which Carl Davis collaborated with Colin Matthews, who by the mid-1980s was becoming very busy.

'Carl asked if I could do it,' says Matthews. 'He thought it would suit me. He wanted something quite aggressive and different, so we devised an orchestra consisting of metal percussion, brass and wind. We thought it would lend an appropriately raucous, primitive kind of sound. We weren't intending to use strings at all, but the producer said, "You can't have a movie score without strings!" We had to divide the recording sessions into sections, so that the whole orchestra wasn't on stand-by. Some sections were for what we called our "barbaric orchestra", the rest were for normal orchestra. Then at the end, the producer admitted, "You were right first time!" So we went back and rescored huge portions in the original style that we had envisaged. It was all right for me, as I got paid twice over. Unfortunately the movie bombed. That was my first experience of the commercial film world, and it was disconcerting. A week later, John Barry phoned up to ask if I would help him with a James Bond film score, and I actually said no! I felt I couldn't devote any more time to films. So my claim to fame is that I turned down the chance to work on a Bond movie!'

Carl Davis admits that *King David* was a flop. It was much derided, and Richard Gere got a Golden Raspberry Award for Worst Actor. 'But for me it was an incredible opportunity. I used psalms as the basis of the score, and I got to set *The Lord is My Shepherd*. There was a great deal of ceremony and dancing in it – at one point David has to dance naked before the altar. Unfortunately the choreography was completely inappropriate, and the producer simply couldn't get to grips with the music requirements. There was supposed to be a large children's choir, which hadn't been booked, and in desperation I got my two young daughters to come into the studio, so that we could at least make a guide track. I told them to sing, and we would double them up and multi-track it. They learned the song, and like true pros they got on with it. At the time the cast was filming in a remote town in Basilicata, and apparently Richard, when he was played the recording of the children's voices, said, "They sound very English!" Richard himself recorded some of the psalms at the Olympic Studio next to our house in Barnes, but except for the orchestra tracks, they weren't used. It was a botched job in many ways. But Richard was often in our house, which was very thrilling, and generously signed many autographs.

'There's a tradition that you preview films before an audience. Bruce rang up to say they had previewed *King David*, and that the producer, Martin Elfand, was furious. I asked why? And he replied: "Because everybody loved the music!"'

The late 80s and 90s

In just one month in 1988, Davis found himself working on three film scores simultaneously – *Scandal*, *The Rainbow*, and *Girl on a Swing*, a supernatural thriller based on a Richard Adams novel which starred, among others, his wife Jean Boht. That was a good month, he recalls. *Scandal*, directed by Michael Caton-Jones, dealt with the revelations that rocked the Macmillan government in 1963 when details emerged about a brief affair two years earlier between John Profumo, Minister of State for War, and would-be model Christine Keeler, played in the film by Joanne Whalley. John Hurt starred as Stephen Ward, the osteopath and socialite who befriended Keeler and her friend Mandy Rice-Davies, and ended up as the real victim of the scandal, killing himself when he was about to be prosecuted for living off the immoral earnings of prostitutes. Davis thinks he once almost met Stephen Ward. 'In 1961 I was living in Notting Hill, in a Rachman slum, and two streets away, just off Portobello Road, there was a marvellous West Indian coffee bar, with a fabulous chef. The proprietors of the "Fiesta" also played the latest jazz LPs, which I soaked up, along with the chilli, paella, ackees and salt cod. Below it, in the basement, was a rather dodgy blue-beat club, where the music competed with the jazz being played upstairs. One night I was eating in the café, when I saw sitting in the window an immaculately suited man, accompanied by two young women with fashionable beehive hair-dos. That was Stephen Ward. Many years later, in 1988, I was offered the film, and while I was working on it I met the real Christine Keeler, who occasionally visited the set, accompanied by her young son. But what scuppered *Scandal* for me was that EMI offered the production the use of any songs from their catalogue. That meant that I was more or less out of the picture – I couldn't possibly compete with Frank Sinatra singing *Witchcraft*!

'On the other hand, I was thrilled to be working on *The Rainbow* with Ken Russell. In the early sixties, when I was living in my West London slum room, I had tried to get involved with *Women in Love*, which is the sequel to *The Rainbow* and was one of the best films that Russell made. I really wanted to write for a D. H. Lawrence subject – I believed I could give it the emotional punch it needed.

'Russell was notorious for tearing up scores, but he was very kind to me. He had seen *Napoléon*, and by 1988 I already had a repertoire of at least twelve silent film scores, many of which Russell had seen at the London Film Festival. He knew a lot about me. We got on well on a personal level, and he paid me the greatest compliment. When I was playing through the score on the piano, there's a scene where the heroine is riding on her bike to an amorous assignation with her teacher. Russell turned to me and said: "You know, if you want the music to go on longer there, I've got more footage. I really like the music, and I've got some more film." That was a very unusual thing for a director to say. I was very flattered, and it turned out to be a good experience.

'Ken Russell was responsible for kick-starting Christopher Gable's acting career. After he had stopped dancing, Russell cast him as Ursula's father in *The Rainbow*. The next time I saw Gable, he was in a studio with Gillian Lynne choreographing my ballet *A Simple Man*.'

In 1994 Davis composed the score for another John Irvin film. *Widows' Peak* was set in Ireland, and starred Natasha Richardson, Mia Farrow, Joan Plowright, Adrian Dunbar and Jim Broadbent. None of the leading ladies was Irish, although Maureen O'Sullivan had originally been asked to play the character of Miss O'Hare, but turned it down in favour of her daughter Mia Farrow. Davis gave his title-music a silvery, delicate timbre, very lightly scored, which suited the subtle atmosphere of this domestic comedy. He also took the opportunity to score a lively scene of Irish folk-dancing, as well as the band at a local fair. 'I loved doing *Widows' Peak,* and I tried to give the music a Celtic flavour. It was very modal, and I created a little suite out of it. The film was well received critically and it won Best Picture at the 1995 Austin Film Festival – but maybe it didn't do quite as well as it should have done.'

Then in 1999, to Davis's great delight, Mike Leigh rang to ask if he would work on *Topsy Turvy* – the story surrounding the creation of *The Mikado*, perhaps the greatest of Gilbert & Sullivan's Savoy Operas. 'I loved Mike's early films – *Abigail's Party, Nuts in May* – they were adorable. I had worked with Mike previously, first of all just on a 30-second trailer for a series of plays on Thames TV. Then in 1977, he asked if I would work with him and producer David Rose on a play for the BBC drama department at Pebble Mill in Birmingham. That was the making of Mike. The first play was called *The Kiss of Death.* It was set in a northern city where one of the characters worked for an undertaker. The strong regional accents made much of it quite unintelligible to me, but working with Mike was absorbing. We spent a lot of time trying to decide on the right sound. He sometimes liked the music to do the opposite of the action.'

In 1982 Davis worked on another Mike Leigh film, *Home Sweet Home,* which was about a group of postmen and their families living on a village housing estate. Said to be 'Leigh's loneliest film', it claimed to be about 'postmen, parenthood, social workers and sex', but it was really about emotional isolation. Davis says the film caused quite a stir. 'I needed to find an odd sound, and settled on a quartet of double-basses. They had difficulty playing it, but it worked well.

'Then after a very long time – seventeen years – Mike rang about *Topsy Turvy.* Who would have thought that he was a Gilbert & Sullivan fan? He surprised everyone. I had loved Gilbert & Sullivan from childhood on – it was part of my image of England.

I can see now that at that time, I wasn't reading them correctly. But by then I was viewing them very differently, having already conducted some concert performances of the repertoire – *HMS Pinafore* and *Trial by Jury* with the Bournemouth Symphony Orchestra and *The Mikado*, *Pinafore* and *Iolanthe* with the Hallé. So I was delighted when Mike asked me to work on *Topsy Turvy*. I conducted the actual G&S numbers for the recording, but I also created a background score. Mike said at our first meeting that he didn't want me to use any Sullivan in that. But by the time he'd shot the film, he said he only wanted Sullivan! I found some really interesting stuff, not all done with Gilbert.

'What I liked most in the film was one scene that I thought was very revealing about the music business. Gilbert and Sullivan are at the height of their success. They need a new operetta, but can't agree on a subject. Gilbert has written a scenario called 'The Mountebanks', about a magic elixir. Sullivan hates it, he thinks that trick has been pulled too many times, and he feels the partnership has run out of steam. They're stuck, and there's a scene between Gilbert, Sullivan and D'Oyly Carte, when Sullivan complains he is not been taken seriously, he wants to write a proper opera. D'Oyly Carte tells him that if he will consent to do another operetta, then he might consider the opera. The camera cuts to Sullivan, and you see his eyes go completely dead. I thought that was perfect. His thinking is entirely internalised. Then the film cuts to Gilbert's study, where the samurai sword falls off the wall, and the idea for *The Mikado* is born.'

Carl Davis's latest film scores have been for two films directed by his eldest daughter, Hannah. He says he gets on famously with his daughters. 'I find them so much fun. Hannah and Jessie are not at all alike as personalities, but both are very outgoing characters. Hannah was a jobbing actress, she went to the Neighborhood Playhouse in New York when she was eighteen, and studied at The Academy in Whitechapel. She had a small part in Mike Leigh's *Secrets and Lies*, and she was in *The Bill*. When she was in her early twenties she met a young actor and writer, David Law.

He was already beginning to write screenplays, and they decided they would try to make films. They did some documentaries, and then Jean and I helped them make their first film, *Mothers and Daughters*, in 2004. It included major parts for themselves and their friends. Then they moved to New York, where in 2008 they got funding from the British Council to make a second film, *The Understudy*. They shot it in a small theatre off Broadway. It's about a talented actress who is always the understudy, and when she finally gets her chance to play a lead, the play is re-cast. Then mysteriously, Hitchcock-like, all the people who have performed the role die – and no one knows whether their deaths are intentional, and whether the understudy is responsible. It's rather ambiguous. Hannah's films are very dark. And of course they asked me to do the scores for them. I say that they don't have to ask me, but they do!

'Hannah and David have now gone off to Hollywood to try their luck. They did manage to sell their two films to various networks, and they are out on DVD. Now they are trying to get their third feature made, so hopefully we shall soon see what emerges.'

VII

BALLET MUSIC

Carl Davis has had a long love affair with ballet. 'I always wanted to write ballet scores. It seemed quite clear by my mid-teens that I couldn't sing, I didn't really have a voice. I would have liked to have been a great tenor, but my voice had no quality. But I thought I would like to dance instead, so very conspiratorially I bought a pair of tights. One day when everyone was out of the house, I thought, "OK, I'm going to change into these tights." Then I stood in front of the mirror, and thought, "No." So there I was, I had no voice, and my body was certainly not a dancer's body. I once told this story to Derek Deane – I was quite drunk at the time, I think it was a birthday party – and he said: "But you never had a class!" It had never occurred to me that with proper training, it might have been possible to change and develop.

'Then I thought: "Well, even if I can't do it myself, I can make people sing, I can make people dance!" A couple of years later when I started composing, I realised that if I could write songs, I also could write musicals, and I could create ballets – and it has moved through in a straight line. That initial desire to *do* it became the desire to *make* it. In a way conducting is the same – it's all about making things happen.'

In fact, it wasn't until the late 1970s that Davis had the chance to tackle ballet. His subsequent career as a ballet composer – he has written thirteen, with another under way – has been consistent with his activities in TV and film. In many ways, the techniques involved are similar. Both media involve visual images and movement, and require precision and split-second timing on the part of the composer. In his opinion: 'The concept of the Wagnerian *Gesamtkunstwerk*, in which all the arts are brought together to the highest level – utilising the best music, the best design concept, décor, costumes, choreography, to create a unique art form, which to a certain extent is also realised in the world of film – involves all the arts working together, usually under the vision of one person. And perhaps the greatest exemplar of such a visionary impresario was Serge Diaghilev.'

Davis has long been fascinated with the story of Diaghilev and the Russian Ballet. 'In the 1940s and '50s there were still people around who had been associated with Diaghilev, and some of his designs were still available – you could still see *Petrushka* in New York as reproduced by Fokine. Diaghilev's 1909 version of *Les Sylphides* was in every major company's repertoire. The Ballets Russes – Diaghilev, the dancers, the designers, the composers – had all been part of my intellectual life since childhood. I was obsessed with the subject, and had read widely around it. I had an uncle – my mother's brother – who was very in touch with the graphic world, and one of my earliest childhood memories was of going through their library of art books, and finding drawings of Nijinsky by Rodin. Rodin wanted to make a sculpture of Nijinsky, but apparently Diaghilev was terribly jealous and after just one sitting prevented Nijinsky from going again.'

One of Carl Davis's first jobs when he came to England in 1960 had been as rehearsal pianist for Western Theatre Ballet, a Bristol-based ballet company run by Elizabeth West and Peter Darrell, which was the precursor of Scottish Ballet. The first ballet that Davis was asked to play for, *Carnaval,* had a Nijinsky connection. It was based on Schumann's music, orchestrated by a quartet of Russian composers – Glazunov, Rimsky-Korsakov, Lyadov and Tcherepnin – and originally choreographed by Fokine, with costumes by Bakst. The great Russian ballerina Tamara Karsavina had created the role of Columbine for the St Petersburg premiere, with Leonid Leontiev as Harlequin, but a couple of months later it was presented by the Ballets Russes in Berlin with Lydia Lopokova as Columbine, and Nijinsky as Harlequin. Karsavina herself, at a great age, had coached some of the Western Theatre Ballet dancers. 'I was horrified when we got to the *Papillons* variation, which is incredibly difficult,' Davis recalls. 'I murdered it! The set was very simple – they had just a long settee, and they danced on it.'

Nijinsky: God of the Dance

Over half a century later, Davis jumped at the chance of writing a ballet based on the life of Nijinsky. The idea was originally mooted in the 1990s, at Northern Ballet Theatre. 'This was an idea that Christopher Gable wanted to do,' says Davis. 'We went to talk to a dramaturg called Patricia Doyle, who had done a lot of research on Nijinsky, and even drafted a scenario.' 'I wanted to learn about this amazing man,' writes Patricia Doyle. 'His fate increasingly moved me – the fate of a man who was very gifted and yet so shy and vulnerable and who lost everything including at last his mind. I'm not religious, but when I think of a Nijinsky ballet the words spirit and soul come to mind.' But, according to Davis, nothing came of it at the time. 'Gable died, and the board of Northern Ballet Theatre said they didn't really think it would be of interest to their audiences. So the whole thing went to sleep. But then the Slovak National Ballet company, based in Bratislava, licensed the Northern Ballet Theatre's production of *Romeo and Juliet*, and took on NBT's ballet master, Brazilian-born Daniel de Andrade. Daniel was asked by the Bratislava company if there was anything he'd like to do, and he suggested Nijinsky.'

Since Davis and Patricia Doyle had been part of the original negotiations, they were taken on board when the commission was finally sealed in 2015. For Patricia Doyle, 'The theme of Nijinsky is a challenge and a hard battle, and for a modern audience it is the chance to rediscover the genius, the dazzling force of the Ballets Russes at its inception, and the lasting effect it has had on the soul and spirit of dance.' The theme was perfect for Davis. 'I had already been thinking a great deal about Nijinsky, and then when this commission came up, I already had the full ammunition. Before, we had never got further than talking, but now there were deadlines, decisions that I had to make. I had read widely about Nijinsky – it was a subject covered by so many people from all points of view – audiences, musicians, patrons, the dancers themselves. It's terrific, how stimulating people found it. So many distinguished people were associated with the Ballets Russes – Cocteau, Picasso, Stravinsky, to name but a few.'

Nijinsky's stellar career was very brief. The greatest male dancer of the early twentieth century, at a time when the spotlight was firmly focused on *prima ballerinas* such as Anna Pavlova, he quickly became famed for his extraordinary virtuosity and charismatic interpretations. He first danced with the Imperial Ballet of St Petersburg as a young graduate of its ballet school in 1907. Two years later he joined Diaghilev's Ballets Russes, starring in the company's early Paris seasons, and choreographing new works such as Debussy's *L'après-midi d'un faune* and Stravinsky's *Le sacre du printemps*. In 1913 Nijinsky led the company on a disastrous South American tour – Diaghilev, who was his lover as well as mentor, refused to go as he was terrified of travel by sea – and while on tour, he married, much to Diaghilev's fury. Nijinsky was dismissed from the company. He spent the first half of the First World War in Switzerland, but by then he was already showing signs of schizophrenia. His last public performance was in 1919, and he spent the remaining three decades of his life in and out of mental institutions. His diaries were originally published in an expurgated version by his wife, Romola, and more recently, the unexpurgated version has been discovered and published. Some incidents in Davis's new ballet – such as Nijinsky's flirtation with six Paris prostitutes in Act II – are based on those diaries.

Nijinsky: God of the Dance is framed by Nijinsky's incarceration in a mental asylum, with incidents from his dancing career occurring within that frame, as if in flashback. The Prologue opens with a single spotlight focusing on a figure crumpled in a chair, facing the audience. Nijinsky is recalling his final performance, in 1919, when he made a charity appearance for the Red Cross in a grand hotel ballroom in St Moritz. His internal distress at the carnage of the Great War is projected in words the wall behind him, and spoken: 'We're at war, the world is in some terrible state of terrifying confusion and we do not know where it will end.' The music for his last performance is the Chopin Prelude No. 20 in C minor, lasting just 16 bars. He unfolds a red cross made from silken strips, lays them on the floor, stands in the middle, and makes just four repeated movements with his arms - out, up, side to side, down.

The whole ballet is built from that initial theme. It begins with a set of formal variations, and then the theme mutates, becoming a waltz, a love theme and a mazurka, reminding the audience of Nijinsky's Polish roots. It recurs at critical points in the story. The first act recalls Nijinsky's early life – his father deserting his mother (herself a dancer), leaving her with three children, of whom the eldest boy Stassik is brain-damaged after suffering a fall. Vaslav and his sister Bronislava enter the ballet school in St Petersburg, and on his graduation day he dances the Blue Bird – one of his signature roles, in which he showed off his famously difficult *entrechat brisée*. The technical demands on the dancer taking the role of Nijinsky are formidable, but the Bratislava ballet company is fortunate in having several Russian-trained dancers who can cope with the moves – the difficulty is finding one who can combine virtuosity with the necessary poetic edge. Act One continues with the birth of the Ballets Russes, Nijinsky's introduction to Diaghilev and his seduction by the impresario, and ends with the company preparing to leave Russia for Paris.

The National Theatre in Bratislava, where the ballet was premiered, is home to an opera company and a theatre company as well as the ballet company. Carl Davis says that he was offered the use of the opera company's chorus, who were kicking their heels in the autumn of 2015. 'I remembered that one of my first professional experiences had been to prepare Ravel's *Daphnis et Chloé* for the Shaw Chorale, and there's a tradition in French music of a female chorus, for instance in Debussy's *Sirènes* and *La demoiselle élue*, as well as in *Daphnis*. So I thought, "What if I turned the Faune into *Daphnis et Chloé*?" doubling the orchestral writing with a wordless chorus in the style of *Daphnis*. It worked perfectly. French composers were greatly influenced by Russian music, so in Act One, after Diaghilev has declared that his ballet company is going to take Paris by storm, the curtains open at the back, and there is a chorus of 80 in golden robes singing the Coronation Scene from *Boris Godunov* as Nijinsky is crowned Tsar of the Ballet. I call that "*The Producers*' moment"!'

Davis's score for *Nijinsky* draws on a mixture of different styles and periods – from classical nineteenth-century ballet music, especially *Giselle*, which Nijinsky danced with Anna Pavlova, through musical modernism to popular South American and jazz idioms of the period, such as tango, samba, ragtime and rumba. The second act recalls pieces from the Ballets Russes repertoire in their glory days in Paris between 1909 and 1913 – music by Tchaikovsky, Chopin, Borodin, Mussorgsky, Rimsky-Korsakov, Ravel and Stravinsky. It is welded together by themes from Rimsky-Korsakov's music for *Scheherezade*, one of Diaghilev's early Parisian triumphs. Davis says that he used the main theme from *Scheherezade* to represent Diaghilev as the Sultan. 'The Rimsky connection was very interesting,' he says. 'It supplies both the seductive theme, and Diaghilev's rage when he heard of Nijinsky's marriage – tearing up posters and throwing sculptures on the floor.' Debussy's haunting flute theme from *L'après-midi d'un faune* – another of Nijinsky's iconic roles – is given to Romola de Pulszky, the Hungarian aristocrat who stalked Nijinsky until he proposed marriage to her. 'It's the essence of sexuality – it accompanies Romola in her swish Paris bathroom, getting ready for an evening at the ballet,' says Davis. The celebrated scarf – which created such a scandal in Nijinsky's hands when the ballet was first performed in 1912 – becomes her scarf. 'Romola's scarf plays a major role. It becomes a love object, and it draws together many musical threads – moving from a French popular *chanson* of the Piaf type into the music of the Faun.'

At a party to raise funds for the company, Nijinsky dances with a guest who is impersonating Charlie Chaplin – a nod to

Carl Davis's filmic preoccupations – and is lured to act out some of his fantasies by a group of French cocottes. He is discovered by Diaghilev, and the two men fight. Act Two ends with a recreation of the celebrated riot which disrupted the opening night of *The Rite of Spring.*

Carl Davis has been obsessed with the creation of *The Rite* since he was a small boy. 'My interest in Stravinsky came from what I was able to read and see – photographs and so on. My parents had a wonderful library which included some books of criticism, and one of them contained a description of the first night of *The Rite of Spring* – the famous riot at the Champs-Elysées Theatre. My first contact with this extraordinary event was in the context of what was reported about it, and some discussion of the significance and the qualities of the score itself – just how new it must have sounded. I didn't see the *Rite* performed on stage until I was living in England. During my research for the *Nijinsky* ballet I must have read fifteen different accounts of the first night, from Marie Rambert's to Misia Sert's. Sert was Diaghilev's best woman friend, and she was always bailing him out financially. She saved the first night of *Petrushka*, when Diaghilev had run out of money. Most people report the response of the audience. Anyone who had any connection to the production wrote about it, but from a very individual point of view.

'I had a problem when I was working on *Nijinsky*. The Stravinsky estate won't allow the score to be touched, and there was no way that we could enlarge our 70-piece orchestra to Stravinsky's 120+ players, just for a five-minute passage dealing with the *Rite*. The way we got round it was that all the first-hand reports said that the music began, and within seconds, you couldn't hear it at all. The racket calmed down a little bit towards the end, because apparently the final solo was so impressive that people stopped yelling, but for the bulk of the performance, no one could hear the music. So I decided there wasn't any point in having much more than the opening bassoon solo, and then we created a riot on tape. I even introduced bits of the *1812 Overture* and the *Marseillaise*, all merged into one terrible noise. There's a famous story of Nijinsky standing in his bathrobe in the wings counting out loud for the dancers, and in my ballet I wanted to have somebody counting in Russian against the background of the riot. Some of the earlier scenes use sections from Stravinsky's own four-hand piano reduction of *The Rite*.

'One of the most mystifying reports from the actual first night was of a man standing up in the audience, shouting "Un dentiste! Un dentiste!" and then another standing up and shouting, "Deux dentistes! Deux dentistes!" and getting attacked by a woman wielding an umbrella. I couldn't understand what all this dentist stuff was about – it seemed utterly absurd. But then one night I was sitting in the Birmingham Hippodrome with David Bintley, watching the Birmingham Royal Ballet in a reconstruction of Nijinsky's original production of *The Rite of Spring*. And at that moment I understood the reference to dentists. When the young girls enter, knock-kneed and pigtailed, they all have their heads on one side pillowed on their folded hands, looking as if they might have toothache! Suddenly it all made sense. Seeing the Birmingham production made me realise just how extraordinary the piece is.

'There were four ballets on the programme at the Paris premiere. The first was *Les Sylphides*, then came *The Rite of Spring*! There's no wonder that the audience found the choreography of *The Rite of Spring* shocking, especially in the context of what they had just seen. The third ballet was *Le spectre de la rose*, danced by Nijinsky, and the fourth was the Polovtsian Dances from *Prince Igor*, for which they had an entire Russian chorus milling about backstage. What struck me so forcibly at the Birmingham performance was the sheer explosion of colour, the excitement of it. French productions at that time were rather misty – you think of *Pelléas*, for example – whereas the Russian Ballet exploded with primary colours, blocks of red, yellow and blue. When you see these original productions, such as the Dutch National Ballet's beautiful, Benois-designed *Petrushka*, you realise how the concept, the choreography, the design, the score, all have equal weight, and all contribute to the experience. My own goal is to create a new ballet work in the most complex form. Influenced by film and theatre as well as ballet music, I want to bring together all the elements that make it powerful, poignant and riveting.'

Act Two of *Nijinsky: God of the Dance* ends with Nijinsky appearing in his rose-petal costume in *Le spectre de la rose* and executing one of his celebrated leaps. Act Three opens with the company boarding the ship that will take them to South America in 1913. At a fancy-dress party on board, during which the company dance a tango and a samba, Nijinsky proposes to Romola, who is now in the company. They are married on arrival in Buenos Aires. When Diaghilev, who is in Venice, hears the news, he is furious, and writes a letter of dismissal to Nijinsky. Rejected by his mentor, out of work, and horrified by the barbarity of the First World War, Nijinsky's sanity begins to disintegrate, and he attacks the servant who brings him his infant daughter. He is confined to a straitjacket in a sanatorium. In the Epilogue, he begins to reprise some of his greatest roles, including Petrushka, the tragic clown, while concluding his opening speech: 'I am God, and all I want is to live in beauty.' The other patients encircle and hail him, as he is showered with rose petals.

Nijinsky: God of the Dance was premiered in Bratislava on 27 November 2015, and has been a great success. It is Carl Davis's thirteenth ballet score.

The Martha Graham connection

Davis's interest in ballet began in childhood. He says that when he was growing up in New York in the late 1930s and 1940s, New York was a magnet for dance. George Balanchine, who was Diaghilev's last choreographer in the late 1920s, was working as the ballet master at New York City Ballet; the Ballet Russe de Monte Carlo was active in New York until 1963; and the American Ballet Theatre was putting on more adventurous productions. Dance was a central factor in every Broadway musical, especially those choreographed by Jerome Robbins and Agnes de Mille. Davis recalls that there was an extraordinary cross-fertilisation of talents. The German expressionist dancer and choreographer

Hanya Holm, who worked in the USA from 1931 onwards and was known as one of the 'Big Four' creators of the American modern dance movement, created the choreography for successful musicals such as *Kiss Me Kate* and *My Fair Lady*. Balanchine himself went to Hollywood in the 1930s and worked on films as well as Broadway musicals, such as the 1939 Rodgers and Hart musical *On Your Toes,* which was the first musical to incorporate classical dance. Many foreign companies visited New York, but on the other hand it was difficult to see a full-length Tchaikovsky ballet there, with the exception of *The Nutcracker.* Balanchine did Act II only of *Swan Lake*, and only Aurora's Wedding was routinely done as an excerpt from *Sleeping Beauty.* Davis says that the 'Americana' side – *Rodeo* and *Billy the Kid* – were the staples of ballet in the US at that time. 'But then you could hear the pieces played on the radio, on a mixed-music schedule, and some of the most significant twentieth-century scores are ballets, particularly the Diaghilev ones. All the orchestras played that repertoire.'

From the age of about nine or ten, Davis began to read books about ballet, as well as criticism in the *New Yorker.* He remembers the first time he saw a ballet, on his eleventh birthday. 'I dragged my parents to it as a birthday present. It was a Ballet Russe de Monte Carlo production of *Giselle* at the Met, with Alexandra Danilova and Frederic Franklin.' During his childhood the Brooklyn Museum, which was about twenty minutes away from the Davis family apartment, used to put on concerts and performances in its Sculpture Court, which had a very fine Egyptian collection. 'My mother took me there. The atmosphere, the smell of it was all-pervading. Jane Dudley, a leading light in the Martha Graham company, had formed a collaborative dance trio with two colleagues in the 1940s, and I saw the trio perform at the Brooklyn Museum. In 1970 Jane Dudley came to England to teach at the London Contemporary Dance School, which had been formed by Robert Cohan, another dancer in Martha Graham's company. Many years later, when my younger daughter Jessie was in her twenties, we went to see the Martha Graham company at the Barbican Theatre, in London. We took my mother, who was by then confined to a wheelchair, and sat near the back. On my right was my mother, and on my left – none other than Jane Dudley! I told Jane that I had seen her all those years ago dancing in the Sculpture Court in the Brooklyn Museum. As we were talking there was a pause, and she said: "And that's when you got turned on to modern dance!"

'Finally I started reading about Martha Graham. She was utterly unique. She had such a long career – she made her New York debut in 1926, and she was seventy-six years old when she gave her last performances in 1969–70. But then she went on to do a string of new ballets, right up to *Maple Leaf Rag*, based on Scott Joplin's music. She was ninety-odd at the time! Very little of Graham was borrowed music. Her ballets almost always had new music, but she did do a version of *The Rite of Spring*, and there was a wonderful Nielsen ballet, *Acts of Light*, that started with the *Helios* Overture. It was magic, with a *Rhinegold*-like opening and a full stage of people.

'There was one fascinating collaboration between Balanchine and Graham – they decided they would do a ballet to the complete orchestral works of Webern, which didn't last more than an hour altogether. So, out of a triple bill, they devised a ballet called *Episodes*, made up from the Op. 21 Symphony; Six Pieces, Op. 6; Five Pieces, Op. 10; Concerto, Op. 24; and the arrangement of the Ricercar from Bach's *Musical Offering*. Graham's modern dance company did a piece in Elizabethan costumes; while Balanchine's New York City Ballet dancers were all dressed in black and white practice clothing. In its original form, Graham danced to the Op. 1 Passacaglia and the Six Pieces, Op. 6, as Mary Queen of Scots. There was a huge block which got turned around to make a throne, and under this block was Graham as the Queen of Scots in a rigidly structured dress in some Elizabethan shape. She teetered towards the edge of the stage and then stepped out of the dress, but the shape of the dress remained on stage. Then the throne was turned over and became the block again, and she mounted it. It was wonderful.

'Dancers nowadays just cross over from one studio to another, alternating between modern dance and classical. This extraordinary mixture of styles is commonplace now, but it wasn't when I was growing up. I saw a lot of dance during my two years at Bard College. I was at the first night of Stravinsky's *Agon* on 1 December 1957. The real sensation was the wonderful black American dancer Arthur Mitchell dancing with whiter-than-white British Diana Adams. Martha Graham used mixed-race dancers all the time, but it wasn't common then in classical ballet. I saw a lot of premieres, including Martha Graham's *Clytemnestra* on 1 April 1958. She choreographed it and danced the title-role. Later I used to bribe a colleague to take my place at New York City Opera rehearsals because I wanted to watch Balanchine rehearsing with the ballet company. He was doing *Symphony in C* – I thought it was so amazing that this piece had been in the repertoire for twenty years, and he was still rehearsing it – but of course the dancers were totally different. They had a wild-card conductor to start with, but then they co-opted a Royal Ballet conductor called Robert Irving who became their principal conductor.

'I was living and breathing dance. It was so exciting. One of the reasons I was drawn to Bard College was that I knew they had a modern dance department, which was run by an important Graham dancer, Jean Erdman. She is still alive – she is now a hundred years old. Jean had created the principal role in *Letter to the World*, Graham's ballet about Emily Dickinson, and I knew she was teaching there. I said I wanted to take some dance classes (not wearing tights!) and to do some choreography. I wrote my first few dance pieces at Bard.'

In fact, Davis did not start to write ballets himself for nearly twenty years, long after he had moved to England. 'My own first ballet was *David and Goliath*, a one-act ballet lasting about 30 minutes. The story was taken from the Bible. It was an interesting collaboration. It was co-choreographed by Robert North, who had studied with and performed for Martha Graham and Merce Cunningham, and Wayne Sleep, who was pure Royal Ballet. Wayne is extraordinary – half dancer, half show-biz. He is physically tiny, but when, as David, he walked towards the audience, he looked unbelievably tall. I used two pianos and percussion and a soprano sax and flugelhorn for the ensemble. *David and Goliath* was created for the London Contemporary Dance Theatre in 1975. It was quite successful, except for one night during its run when for some reason the company suddenly changed the order of the bill. Instead of being second or third, it suddenly became the opening ballet, and the saxophonist hadn't been told, and didn't turn up until it was over.'

Dances of Love and Death

A few years later, in 1981, Davis was asked by the artistic director and principal choreographer of London Contemporary Dance Theatre, Robert Cohan, to work on a full-length ballet, *Dances of Love and Death*. 'It was a sequence of iconic love stories, structured chronologically from Greek myth to the twentieth century. The five individual stories were separated by abstract interludes of pure dance, set to Conlon Nancarrow's music for player piano. New York-born Robert Cohan had been a principal dancer in the Martha Graham Company. I had seen him perform many times in New York and London and loved his work. He was a great influence on the dance world in England, forming both the London Contemporary Dance School and Company in 1967. Our first meeting to discuss *Dances of Love and Death* was interesting. He offered me a choice; he could either choreograph the work first without music, and I would respond to it and then compose; or I could compose the score first and he would choreograph to the music. Astonished, I chose the latter. This way of working is not unusual in today's dance, but then it was quite alien to me. The independence of movement from music I knew from the works of Merce Cunningham and enjoyed.

'Opera, musicals, ballet – they all need a theme. You start with a subject – the bulk of my work has had a theme or a story, although ballets can work without a specific theme, being based more around an emotion. I would class Balanchine as the master of the plotless ballet, but nevertheless it's going to be performed by human beings, and you are going to find themes. So, for instance, if you're writing a slow movement, will it be more of a love theme, or is it tragic? Once a theme has been decided, everyone – composer, designer, choreographer, dancers – is a slave to that theme and works towards expressing it. I always start from the premise that we should talk a lot, I would read a lot, and only then would I start to compose.

'*Dances of Love and Death* consisted of five famous love stories, each of which had to be condensed into about twenty minutes each. Robert hadn't decided what all of them were going to be, so I suggested that they should be historically chronological. We started with the Greek myth of Persephone, and for the second, I dared to suggest Tristan and Isolde. That gave me the opportunity to write something very medieval-sounding, with a big pavane as the central section, and a love scene. For the third section, Robert wanted to do his own version of Sleeping Beauty, in which the princess wakes up from her enchanted sleep, but rejects the prince. She won't marry him until he has gone away and performed further exploits – although they do kiss at the end of Act One. Act Two opened with *Wuthering Heights*, one of the great eternal love stories. Interestingly, I had just written the music for a TV adaptation of the novel, whose principal themes could be redeveloped.

'The last section was about Marilyn Monroe, particularly her love affair with the camera. Linking it all were the mythological figures of Love and Death – they were Venus and Mars. The Venus figure was transformed into Marilyn, onstage. A theatrical dressing-table and mirror was wheeled on, with the famous blonde hairstyle in the form of a wig, and the dancer turned herself into Marilyn in front of the audience, while four men stood around waiting to dance with her. She always kept people waiting!'

A Simple Man

Fast-forward to 1987. Carl Davis and the choreographer Gillian Lynne are sitting at the piano in a rehearsal studio at Northern

Ballet Theatre. Both are despondent. Outside the window, the view is deeply uninspiring – a typical Moss Side slum scene with a row of boarded-up shops, endless blocks of dismal, run-down flats, and little sign of life except for occasional spirals of black smoke where a burning mattress has been thrown from a high balcony. Gillian Lynne is stressed. She is working on two simultaneous projects – Andrew Lloyd Webber's new show *Phantom of the Opera*, and Northern Ballet Theatre's new ballet based on the life of the Lancashire-born painter L. S. Lowry, *A Simple Man*. Gillian, pressed for time, is trying to do the choreography in small, self-contained sections, and she and Davis have reached an impasse. Towards the close of the ballet Lowry is watching a scene he painted over and over again – workers coming home from the mill. Despite Davis's best efforts, the music is not matching Gillian's mental conception of the scene. She puts her head in her hands, and moans to herself, 'Poor Gilly!' In desperation Davis says: 'Just show me something, how you want the characters to be, what you want them to do.'

'OK,' says Gillian, 'let me show you something. This is what I want – it's got to be purposeful and strong. They're tired, but they're going home!' She springs to her feet, moving around the room, spinning and jumping, and improvising a dance. Davis brightens visibly. 'OK, I think I've got it! Give me half an hour and I'll have the 45 seconds of music you need. I'll write it now and I'll play it for you.' Half an hour later, Gillian returns. Davis has come up with a perfect solution. The fog has cleared.

That, he says, was an interesting example of how through cross-stimulation, through discussion and demonstration, you can finally arrive at a solution. 'I find that collaborative way of working very exciting and very fruitful. Of course it's always a gamble – you don't know if it will eventually work out. At that particular point I had nothing clear in my mind, and Gillian showed it to me. I can't work in small individual sections of bars: I need to establish the mood. The music, the emotion, for me is the springboard for the whole thing.'

At this stage Carl Davis's ballet commissions were still widely spaced. In 1986 he had collaborated with the director and producer

Tom Gutteridge on a television ballet, *Fire and Ice*, created for the British Olympic ice-skating champions Jayne Torvill and Christopher Dean. Torvill and Dean were then at the height of their fame, having achieved the highest figure-skating score of all time two years earlier at the Sarajevo Winter Olympics with their stunning performance to Ravel's *Bolero*. *Fire and Ice*, in which the two opposing elements are represented by Dean as a Fire Prince and Torvill as an Ice Princess, was shown on LWT at Christmas 1986. The following year, another TV commission led to Davis's first work for Christopher Gable's Northern Ballet, and his first major success as a composer of ballets.

1987 marked the centenary of the birth of the Lancastrian painter L. S. Lowry, famous for his idiosyncratic depictions of northern industrial landscapes and their working people. To mark the occasion, the City of Salford commissioned a one-act ballet, inspired by Lowry's life and characters from his paintings, from Gillian Lynne and Carl Davis. *A Simple Man* (Lowry's own description of himself) was to be televised as a BBC *Omnibus* programme, performed by Northern Ballet Theatre. It was first performed as a live ballet at the Palace Theatre in Manchester in November 1987. David Wilson's sets and Tim Goodchild's costumes reproduced backdrops and scenes from Lowry's paintings in his distinctive colour palette – shades of white-grey, charcoal, khaki, ochre, and washed-out blues, greens and bisque. The *corps de ballet*, representing the Salford mill-workers depicted by Lowry as stick men and women, adopt exaggerated, unnatural attitudes, moving their elongated limbs jerkily, their faces painted chalk white. Lowry's perception of humanity was unremittingly bleak – he painted real people – sad and unattractive – and he himself was fundamentally lonely. He once said: 'Every human being stands alone in the last extremity. That's the way I see it.' In Gillian Lynne's conception, the figure of Lowry, dressed in a shabby khaki-coloured mackintosh, wanders through the bleak industrial landscape of his own paintings, seeing individuals such as the Father Coming Home Drunk, or the Balloon-Seller, whom he immortalises on canvas. Colour comes into his life in the form of an idealised girl in a scarlet dress, whom he painted as 'Anne' – but the other individual girls in the ballet, who appear in his paintings, may have been fantasy figures – the girl in a tennis dress, brandishing a racquet, and two coquettes with exposed false breasts in bright pink dresses, who represented a hidden, semi-pornographic side of Lowry's art.

At the heart of the ballet lies Lowry's tortured relationship with his mother, with whom he lived until her death in 1939. Lowry, then in his early fifties, and unmarried, was devastated by her death, even though his mother, an aspiring pianist, did not appreciate her son's talent and was perpetually disappointed by him. Their tender *pas de deux*, and her deathbed scene, in which Lowry hauls her bedstead around in his agony and despair, form the core of the ballet.

Carl Davis says that his score was derived from an interesting fact he discovered about how Lowry came to paint in such an idiosyncratic style. 'His emergence as a painter was very gradual, he hardly thought of himself as an artist at all, but due to the influence of his main teacher at the Manchester School of Art, a little-known French Impressionist painter called Pierre Adolphe Valette, Lowry got the idea of setting figures against a white background and he decided to develop that. What made it distinctive was that he repainted his white backgrounds, until there were three layers of white paint; then on the last one, while it was still wet, he would incise his matchstick-like figures, so that they stood out in relief. I thought that this idea of white on white on white had a purity of sound. I liked that idea very much. The whole basis of the ballet was this idea of visualising that discovery, translating it into sound. It seemed to be begging for life.'

Davis's compact and coherent score for *A Simple Man* captures the vigour of Manchester street life – the workers, dressed exactly as Lowry painted them, the men in drab grey suits and flat caps, women in shabby faded dresses – go through the dreary routine of their quotidian existence. Ostinato rhythmic and melodic patterns accompany their daily passage to and from the mills, where they labour to the accompaniment of Soviet-style industrial music heavy with brass. On emerging they and their children surround a balloon seller with a hurdy-gurdy playing a cheap circus waltz with an oom-pah accompaniment; the men get into a fight; the women dance a clog dance in the sheer relief of being released from servitude. The daily grind of their existence is contrasted with the interior world of The Mother and the idealised girls of Lowry's imagination.

Davis's favourite combination of piano and strings bathes The Mother in a romantic, Tchaikovskian aura; while the figure of Anne and her two identical alter egos dance to a fluty, baroque-sounding ensemble. Anne and Lowry dance an awkward *pas de deux* sitting and standing on rigidly opposing chairs, while the music expresses his frustrated longing and her unattainability. She is dismissed by The Mother – the only significant woman in Lowry's life – and in a spectacular *coup de théâtre,* inspired by a particular painting of the beach at Sunderland, Lowry takes his mother for a walk by the North Sea, its shallow breakers represented by dancers slowly rolling in shimmering blue and grey net, to the accompaniment of a Satie-esque flute solo with a gentle ostinato accompaniment.

The second girl of Lowry's imagination, the tennis player, makes an appearance to a French-style café waltz introduced by a violin solo. She and Lowry dance a luminously orchestrated *pas de deux*, but their reverie is interrupted by The Mother's illness, and the mental and musical disintegration of her death, during which Lowry's anguish, depicted in a hideous painting of himself with swollen, red eyes, is mirrored in the increasing dissonance of the musical idiom. Lowry returns to his solitary strolls among a crowd of misfits and oddities, the people through whom he eventually achieves fame, depicting them on canvas exactly as he sees them. At the end of the ballet, he is accosted by one of his subjects, a clown-like figure, who seizes his left arm and raises it in a kind of triumph.

Christopher Gable agreed to come out of retirement as a dancer to play Lowry in *A Simple Man*. Gable had started his career as a principal dancer with the Royal Ballet, before suffering chronic problems with his feet and leaving in 1967 to pursue an acting career. He appeared in several films directed by Ken Russell, before returning to the world of ballet in 1982 as the founder of the Central School of Ballet. And, to Davis's immense delight, Moira Shearer agreed to play Lowry's mother in the TV version. Back in 1948, Shearer had starred in Powell and Pressburger's *The Red Shoes*, the most influential film about ballet ever made. Davis says he remembers begging his parents to take him to see it at a small art cinema in the Broadway area. Later, in the 1950s, he saw Moira dance on stage in New York. 'She then retired, married Ludovic Kennedy, and had her children. Ludovic narrated at some of my concerts and I had met Moira. When the idea of *A Simple Man* came up, and Christopher Gable emerged from retirement to do it, Moira agreed to partner him as The Mother. Although she hadn't danced for forty years, she still looked amazing – her hair was still that wonderful deep auburn colour. But she wouldn't do live performances on stage, and when the ballet entered the repertoire of Northern Ballet – it became their signature ballet, and was much performed – at one point they had Lynn Seymour play The Mother on tour with them. When *A Simple Man* opened at Sadler's Wells, they asked if I would conduct the first night. I ended up taking a curtain call, standing between Lynn Seymour and Christopher Gable, both of whom I remembered seeing in the 1960s when they were the new kids on the block, dancing in Ashton's *The Two Pigeons* and MacMillan's *The Invitation*. I was so overwhelmed with emotion that I rushed forward to take a bow, and suddenly realised I was teetering dangerously close to the edge of the stage. Then I realised that Lynn was holding on to my arm with an iron grip, pulling me back from the brink.'

A Christmas Carol

The success of *A Simple Man*, which won a BAFTA award in 1987, established Davis's career in the ballet world. It also led to Christopher Gable being invited to become the artistic director of Northern Ballet Theatre. From then until his untimely death in 1998, he became a major force in contemporary ballet, and in particular for that company, for which Carl Davis was invited to do three further ballets. The first (also choreographed by Gillian Lynne) was *Lippizaner* (1989), about the famous Viennese dancing stallions; it was followed immediately by an Offenbach ballet called *Liaisons amoureuses*, in which Davis worked with Ronald Hynd, who by then had retired from dancing. 'That was enormous fun,' says Davis. 'It was great to go through almost any operetta by Offenbach. Christopher remarked that all three of us were smiling from the first note. Then that led, three years later, to my biggest success in the ballet field. I was chatting with friends, and asked: "What makes a really successful three-act ballet?" The answer seemed to be that it should be based on a subject that the audience knows well. So I thought about Dickens's *A Christmas Carol*. There are plenty of other adaptations, for film, theatre, and so on, but apparently no ballet. I began work on it, and thought that as a sub-structure I must draw on the rich treasury of English Christmas carols, making sure that they came from the Victorian period. I did slip up a bit – I found out recently that one carol was written later than Dickens. Normally of course, dancers don't sing, but they engaged a vocal coach, and they tried it out. They toured it for about twelve consecutive years, and it was a great success.'

The Picture of Dorian Gray

Coincidentally with Davis's work on *A Simple Man* for Northern Ballet Theatre, in 1987 Derek Deane asked him to do a score for what was to become the Birmingham Royal Ballet, based on Oscar Wilde's ghost story *The Picture of Dorian Gray*. Davis jumped at the chance, particularly as he had recently composed music for a two-part TV series about Oscar Wilde, starring Michael Gambon. 'For me the central excitement, after finding a subject, is establishing the mood of a particular scene – that gives me the impetus I need to write the music. For instance, in *Dorian Gray*, which was my first classical ballet for Derek Deane, there's a backstage scene when Dorian Gray's lover Sybil Vane has just performed Juliet, and comes backstage. Dorian is there, and they perform a *pas de deux*. This was a big lyric scene. At the first rehearsal at Sadler's Wells, we had reached a point at which Sybil has just walked offstage and is going to meet her lover. I shooed the rehearsal pianist away, and said: "I'll play, and show you what it's like." And after listening to the music, Derek indicated what steps he wanted, and the dancer playing Sybil danced it, and we all looked in the mirror to see if it had worked. That to me was the ultimate experience. It satisfied my every desire. I had created the music, and somehow I had envisaged the choreography in my mind while writing it, and it worked. Shape, texture, mood – the music has to express everything. That moment of creation starts there. Then the choreography should soar. The atmosphere and the ambience of the rehearsal room is crucial. In this particular case, the dancer was wearing Juliet's costume, and as it turned out, it was one of Margot Fonteyn's old costumes that she had worn for the Prokofiev ballet. That made it even more thrilling.'

Alice in Wonderland

At that point, Davis began a period of real success in the ballet field. In 1995, Derek Deane, who by then was Artistic Director of English National Ballet, wanted a ballet based on *Alice in Wonderland*. 'I was immersed in the Alice story,' says Davis. 'I had worked on a very elaborate *Alice* musical with John Wells back in the seventies, which had been performed at the Lyric Hammersmith and then at West Yorkshire Playhouse and the Birmingham Rep. It was a lovely adaptation and had quite a successful run. It's a perennial subject and I was still finding amazing nuances and meanings in the story. When Derek said, "I'd like you to do an *Alice in Wonderland* ballet," I thought, "Great!" – and then he said: "But I want the music to be by Tchaikovsky!" My first reaction was unquestionably one of disappointment. At the same time, the other half of me was thinking, "How can I bring this together?" After half an hour or so, I had rationalised this request, and was thinking of a crazy connection. *Alice* was originally published in the 1860s, and was an enormous success. English was spoken at the Russian court: educated Russians spoke English and French, rather than their native language, which was regarded as rather common; and middle- and upper-class children of the time might well have had English governesses. There's every reason to suppose that they might have read *Alice in Wonderland*: it exists in Russian translations. Tchaikovsky wrote a set of piano pieces called *For Children*, full of gorgeous music. They are not designed for children to play – they are too hard – they are intended to be played *to* children. I had this mental image of Lewis Carroll sitting with the little Liddell girls and telling them the story – it's not written in childish language, it's very complex and sophisticated, as are the Tchaikovsky pieces. Those pieces are trying to tell a story; they are highly characterised, with evocative titles. I thought I could use that as a thread connecting Carroll and Tchaikovsky. In the end I used 18 out of the 24 pieces. But the score also had to contain some substantial symphonic movements, for scenes like the Garden of the Talking Flowers. I used the waltz from the Fifth Symphony for that; and the beginning of the fall down the rabbit hole uses music from the symphonic poem *The Tempest*. I also drew on music from the orchestral suites. I really had a lovely time. I found all sorts of connections, and I wanted the audience to believe that Tchaikovsky wrote that music especially for this ballet.'

The Lady of the Camellias

Davis worked again with Derek Deane thirteen years later, in 2008. 'One of the ballerinas at English National Ballet had retired, and had become head of the National Ballet of Croatia, based in Zagreb. She asked Derek if he would go to Zagreb and mount the three Tchaikovsky ballets for her company. Then he asked me if I would do a ballet on the subject of the Lady of the Camellias. I got so excited that I immediately began running a fever, although my identification with the subject-matter didn't quite run to coughing blood! I thought it would be a wonderful and challenging thing to do. I wanted to go back to the original book and the play, which wasn't too successful in the first instance, until Sarah Bernhardt took it up. Verdi saw her perform the leading role in Paris, and was inspired to write *La traviata* afterwards. *The Lady of the Camellias* is a two-act, full-length ballet. They ran it for about three or four seasons in Zagreb. The music is original, except for two delicious places.

'I was very concerned that we shouldn't just do "the ballet of *La traviata*". I consider *La traviata* completely successful as an opera. Back in the 1970s I had already scored a two-part BBC adaptation of the book, with Kate Nelligan as Marguérite and Peter Firth, who had just had a great success in *Equus*, as Armand. There were two points in the book that I particularly wanted to incorporate into the ballet. One where Marguérite is found playing the piano, and one of the pieces she knows is the Weber *Invitation to the Waltz,* but she can only play the easy bits. The other scene is how the lovers meet. One of the functions of a theatre or opera house in the nineteenth century was that courtesans used to ply their trade there. They would be seen, contacts would be made and introductions effected, all quite separate from the dramatic function of the theatre. In the book, Marguérite's first encounter with Armand is at the opera – a friend introduces them. I wondered, did it have to be an opera, perhaps it could be a ballet? *Giselle* is not a bad idea, because of its romantic story in which the heroine dies – there was a neat parallel. So we had them see each other across the theatre from two boxes, while the final scene from *Giselle* is playing out on stage.

'There's a very interesting role which is not developed in Verdi at all. As Marguérite's star dims, she leaves the Paris scene, and another female character, Olympe, rises to take her place. That role, erased from the opera, is important in the ballet: it's at a party thrown by Olympe that the gambling scene takes place, where Armand throws money at Marguérite to humiliate her. We tried to capture the madcap, raucous atmosphere of that world, which Verdi reproduced so well. I thought that Offenbach and Parisian music-hall would be a good starting point.

Carl in Barnes, working with David Gill

From the ballet *The Lady of the Camellias*

Carl with Torvill and Dean

From the ballet *Alice in Wonderland*

Dame Edna Everage, *Last Night of the Poms*, 1983

Carl as the murderous neighbour in Hannah Davis's *The Understudy*

Carl with Sir Paul McCartney at the premiere of the Liverpool Oratorio

Carl on *This Is Your Life*, with Jean

Carl with Jean and
with Diva the dachshund

Left to right Hannah, Carl, Jean (sitting), Jessie, Barney the dog, *c.* 1989

'Then there's a scene at which Armand is packing to leave Paris, and Marguérite arrives. She tells him that she is dying, but she wants to spend one last night with him. He is appalled and nauseated, but excited at the same time. They spend a passionate night together, and in the morning he leaves. In the novel, and my ballet, Marguérite dies alone, without Armand returning to her and apologising, as in the opera. There is no redemption.'

Cyrano

In 2004, Carl Davis had started working on a project based on another French literary classic, Edmond Rostand's 1897 play *Cyrano de Bergerac*. His collaborator this time was David Bintley, the former ballet dancer turned choreographer who in 1995 succeeded Sir Peter Wright as Artistic Director at the Birmingham Royal Ballet. *Cyrano* tells the tragic story of a seventeenth-century soldier-poet who believes that his exceptionally prominent nose renders him so physically unattractive that he is unable to declare his love for his beautiful cousin Roxane, and ends up wooing her by proxy, on behalf of another man. The story has been adapted innumerable times on stage and film, and had even been made into a ballet in 1959 by Roland Petit, with music by Marius Constant. Davis says that the play had been on the family bookshelves in Brooklyn, and he had always been drawn to it. 'Although I saw the 1950s Hollywood film starring José Ferrer and the stunning 1990 French production with Gerard Dépardieu, live stage productions and David Bintley's earlier ballet slipped past my radar. When, in 2004, I was offered the opportunity to compose a new score for David, memories, not so much of the *Cyrano* films, but of my repeated childhood readings of the play, came flooding back.'

Bintley had originally staged *Cyrano* for the Royal Ballet in 1991, with a score by Wilfred Josephs, who was very ill at the time. 'It wasn't a success,' he says. 'It was revived fairly quickly afterwards, and still didn't work, but I had tremendous faith in the idea. People initially thought it was a poor subject for a ballet, but it wasn't.

Then Wilfred died, and we put it aside. With a dormant work there's always the question of what happens to the scenery and costumes, which are expensive to store, and in this case I asked if we could keep them, because at that time (the mid-1990s) the move to Birmingham had come up, and I thought it might give me the possibility of trying *Cyrano* again. We ended up storing them for about fifteen years. In the meantime I thought about changing and adapting Wilfred's score, but it didn't come to anything. Then Sally Cavender at Faber Music sent me a pile of CDs, including some by Carl. He had written lots of music for various ballet companies by then, and I was on the lookout for new composers. I heard that he loved the play, and was really excited by it. I put the CDs on, and suddenly some bits of music that he'd written for various things seemed to be saying, "That's Cyrano!" One of the hardest sections to get right for *Cyrano*, which hadn't worked at all in Josephs' score, was the music that accompanies the man falling from the moon. But there was one piece that Carl had written for the Torvill and Dean ballet *Fire and Ice*, scored for ondes martenot, that I thought would work perfectly. I said, "I want that piece!"'

'David rang me up, and suggested we should meet,' says Davis. 'He felt that the previous version of *Cyrano* had been too fragmentary, as he had tried to include every single scene of the play. He wasn't happy with the score, and Josephs had been too ill to make substantial changes. David felt that he was stuck, and that some of the problems attached to the first production were due to a lack of flexibility in the music. But he thought it was an important work, and he wanted to revive it. The original costumes were opulent, and David wanted to keep those. He was also waiting for the right dancer in the title role to come along.'

'The amazing thing about Carl is that he's so knowledgeable about dance,' says David Bintley. 'He knows so much about it because he's an enthusiast. His instincts are always really good. He writes dance music – in fact it's virtually impossible to stop him writing dance music! He moves into a mode where every piece of music has a dance rhythm, and in some respects a dance structure as well. He has an innate feel for how classical dance music is phrased. With other composers, you often have to give them a crash course in how dance music, and particularly classical dance, works.

'I start by constructing a detailed scenario, with specific time-slots for the individual solos and so on. If you're working with an inexperienced ballet composer, they don't know how long pieces should be, unless they are working to very specific scenarios. Arthur Bliss composed a six-minute solo for a male dancer in *Checkmate*, because he'd never written a ballet before and didn't know any differently! The great thing about Carl is that through his experience and his knowledge, he knows precisely how long a male solo or a female solo should be. He would write the piece to a time-slot, and I would get the recording and listen to it, and if it was right, I would either say, "Great, that works", or "It would be nice if that bit built up more there", or "Perhaps it should be more reflective in the middle." I would give him feedback.'

'If a choreographer says to a composer: "It's too long", or "It's too short", you have to pay attention,' says Carl Davis. 'David and I developed a wonderful working relationship.'

'There were occasions where we had a disagreement over something or other,' says Bintley, 'when Carl reluctantly gave up and said, "If it doesn't work, it doesn't work." I think Carl actually enjoys it when things go wrong, and he has to write or re-write something overnight. And whereas that would be a major problem for most musicians, Carl just gets on and does it. Working with Carl made me realise that it's much better to admit that something doesn't work, than to live and regret it. That changed me a lot. You have to go with that gut feeling.

'Carl's experience and knowledge, plus the fact that much of his music has a nineteenth-century consciousness about it, made me realise that he was the right man for *Cyrano*. He writes the kind of music I'm expecting. It was the opposite with Wilfred Josephs. His score failed because it wasn't a dance score. I had to keep saying to him, "I need the rhythm." But I didn't have enough experience at the time to be able to get that from Wilfred.

'Carl taught me so much. One thing was "don't stop dancing". It may sound obvious, but people who come to see ballet want to see people dancing. If in doubt, dance! It took me a long time to learn that. I once did another ballet which had very little dancing in the overture, which lasted about 10 minutes. It killed the production from the start. After working with Carl, I went back to the composer and asked him to rewrite the whole of the first section, and that turned it around. I learned that from Carl.

'Cyrano starts with a play within a play – I took a leaf out of "legitimate" theatre, and had the people in the onstage theatre arriving in tandem with the actual audience in the real theatre. When both audiences have arrived, and are chatting quite noisily, as audiences do, a man comes out, strikes the stage with his stick three times, as they used to do in the Baroque era to signal the start of a performance, and the music begins as the chandelier rises. That worked perfectly well in London and Birmingham. Everywhere else in the country, as soon as someone walked on to the stage, they all shut up. In Salford, the audience watched the dancers on the stage in total silence. I think we may have to change that when we revive it.

'Carl's score for Cyrano really worked. What was really good about the whole experience was that we turned around something that had been a failure. If we'd had to make the sets and costumes from scratch, it would have cost us a least half a million pounds. I'm glad I kept my faith in the project.'

'I had one niggling doubt about Cyrano,' says Davis. 'The subject of the play is eloquence. Can words be translated into movement? The play is intrinsically about an incredibly articulate man wooing the woman he truly loves on behalf of his friend, who is unable to express anything in words. That's a very difficult concept to put across in dance. There's one scene where the heroine, Roxane, is sitting with the man she has a crush on and who loves her in return, but he can't express what he feels about her. That's all about words. But David's choreography managed to convey it brilliantly – we called it our "Don't speak pas de deux".'

Of all Davis's full-length ballet scores, Cyrano, which was first staged by the Birmingham Royal Ballet in 2007, bears the strongest relationship to the kind of dramatic scores he employs for silent cinema. While paying lip-service to the Baroque setting of the play – particularly in the opening French overture and minuet in 'The Chandelier Rises', and a delicately scored pavane danced by Roxane and Christian in Act III – the music is rooted firmly in the Romantic idiom, with a distinctly French twist (echoes of Offenbach, the Bizet of *L'Arlésienne*, and Delibes). The richly textured score incorporates full-blown love themes, marches and elegant waltzes: one such, introduced by a Tchaikovskian violin solo, accompanies a duelling scene. There are lively dances such as the regimental *Rataplan* with its imitation of the *tambour militaire* and the swirling nuns' dance in Act III with a folk-like central section; a lilting passepied, a French farandole and Spanish-style habaneras, as well as a Mozartian serenade – played on trombone – with a guitar-like accompaniment on pizzicato strings. Cyrano's ethereal Moon Dance is accompanied by the unearthly sound of the *ondes martenot*.

Cyrano's regiment of hot-headed Gascon cadets (noblemen-soldiers) is defined by the 'swashbuckling' idiom familiar from some of Davis's silent-film scores. On the one hand Cyrano's famous 'panache' (meaning both the white plume in his hat, and his reputation for flamboyant style and reckless courage) is represented by trumpet fanfares; the red rose that Roxane gives him (a symbol of hope) by a theme with an Elgarian twist and the poetic side of his nature by a lyrical cello solo underpinned by harp, which runs through the score. All three themes, as well as the *Moon Dance*, return to poignant effect during his death scene. Even his nose – the fateful impediment to his amorous success – has an appropriately ominous theme. Christian's dyslexia is initially portrayed by a hesitant waltz, and then by a solo clarinet. His love scenes with Roxane, actually conducted by his proxy, Cyrano, are characterised by tender solos for cello (the disguised voice of Cyrano) and violin (Christian), which blossom into an ecstatic love theme. The theme associated with Roxane, first heard on flute accompanied by pizzicato strings, returns on attenuated violins in the ballet's final scene (*Roxane Alone*) when she realises, too late, that she has loved Cyrano all along.

Aladdin

David Bintley also revived a previous work of Davis's, which had fizzled out after a successful premiere eight years previously. *Aladdin*, a full-length, three-act ballet based on a story from *1001 Nights,* was commissioned in 2000 by Scottish Ballet, which had grown out of the Western Theatre Ballet company for which Davis had acted as rehearsal pianist on *Le Carnaval*, back in 1960. Under its inspirational choreographer Peter Darrell, the company had thrived and had relocated to Glasgow from Bristol.

'Sometime in the 1990s,' says Davis, 'I had a phone call from Robert Cohan. I had not really been in contact with him much since the 1980s when we had worked together on *Dances of Love and Death*. In the interim Robert had retired from the London Contemporary Dance Company, but continued to guest choreograph chiefly for Scottish Ballet, now under the direction of Galina Samsova. I had known Galina as principal ballerina with the Sadler's Wells Ballet, where she had played an important role in Derek Deane's *Dorian Gray*. It may have been she who suggested the idea of *Aladdin* as a ballet – it is the UK's most popular pantomime – but she certainly played an important role in its conception. I saw in *Aladdin* the possibility of a truly popular, entertaining, family-orientated ballet, a possible alternative to the perennial *Nutcracker.*'

All looked set for success, but then ill fortune intervened. Scottish Ballet and the Scottish Arts Council found themselves locked in a struggle over both artistic policy and finances, with the company obliged to manage on a diminishing budget. 'Things looked bad for *Aladdin*,' says Davis. 'Then in 1999, Robert North, with whom I had worked on *David and Goliath* many years ago, was appointed artistic director of Scottish Ballet and immediately reinstated *Aladdin* into the schedule. But disaster struck again. After a successful opening in Glasgow on 6 February 2001, followed by a tour, the next season's tour – already booked – was abruptly cancelled. Scottish Ballet was to shrink in size to around twenty dancers and become a contemporary dance company, rendering further performances of *Aladdin* impossible.

'Happily I was able to rescue the score. From 2003 I had established a marvellous relationship with the newly formed Malaysian Philharmonic Orchestra, performing my silent-film scores and themed concerts. They offered me their orchestra and hall in Kuala Lumpur for a full recording of *Aladdin* in 2005. At that time I was working on *Cyrano*, and on the off-chance sent a CD of *Aladdin* to David Bintley. To my delight, I had a quick response: "I think I can do something with it but I don't know when or where." The "when" turned out to be 2008, the "where" was Tokyo, and the company was the National Ballet of Japan, where David was co-artistic director.'

'I have a joke that Carl saved my *Cyrano*, so I saved his *Aladdin*,' says David Bintley. 'Carl was rather proud of his piece, and had recorded it with his Malaysian orchestra. While we were working on *Cyrano* he gave me a recording, which wasn't professionally produced at that point. The idea of doing an Aladdin ballet didn't interest me – too many pantomimes! But then I thought I should listen to it, so I put it on in the car while I was driving from Milton Keynes to Salford. It took the full length of the journey. I parked the car and rang him up, and said, "Carl! *Aladdin*! It's wonderful!" And Carl said, "I know!" That was so typical of Carl. But I absolutely loved it. It *was* wonderful. It's the most charming, delightful, trouble-free piece, and I said I wanted to do it somewhere. I did it in the perfect place – Japan – with the perfect company, at exactly the right time. It was a great experience from beginning to end. I remember bringing it back to Birmingham and wondering, "What are they going to think?" But what's wrong with something that is just fun, and charming? People adore Gilbert and Sullivan, but they never pretended to be Wagner. I love *Aladdin* from beginning to end. There are no clouds in the sky, and we know it's going to end well. It's so redolent of nineteenth-century Orientalism, and Carl's original music captured that atmosphere perfectly. The critics were sniffy – I think one of them declared that there was too much dancing in it! How do you figure *that* out? But the company really took to it. It offers so many opportunities for the cast, there are lots of cameos. The whole score just dances.'

Aladdin is a feast of visual and aural riches, of dazzling costumes and dramatic sets, including one scene in a souk hung with carpets and another set in a desert with a huge, rising red sun: an *Arabian Nights* fantasy of minarets and oriental palace interiors, with a flying carpet, a Djinn of the Lamp who appears in a puff of blue smoke, and a huge pantomime dragon. At its heart is the love story between the street urchin Aladdin and the princess Badr al-Badur – one critic described it as 'Romeo and Juliet re-located to the souk' – and their *pas de deux* are firmly rooted in classical ballet, well suited to the kind of expansive themes Davis uses in his film music. His score also incorporates exotic elements to conjure up the ballet's locations in Persia, China and North Africa: music built over a Middle-Eastern sounding bass drone to represent Aladdin's Lamp, use of the pentatonic scale, traditional Chinese dances such as the Lion Dance and the Dragon Dance, and North African drumming. David Bintley says that the original scenario incorporated quite a lot of stage magic which was later cut, including a clever trick in which Aladdin escapes with the magic ring, apparently vanishing into thin air. 'It took about five minutes – too long to do.

'*Aladdin* is set in the fantasy China of the Arabian Nights,' Bintley says. 'The Japanese have a strange relationship with the Chinese – the political enmity goes back a long way, so we had to tread carefully. Their knowledge of *Aladdin* comes from the Disney film, which isn't really set in China, but in an all-purpose Middle East, a fantasy Persia. I had to tread that strange ground between *Aladdin* being Chinese, and yet not being Chinese. But Carl's music, especially the big love theme, was resolutely pentatonic, and sounds Chinese. So we made the characters immigrants, and created a little corner of China in Baghdad – an exotic Aladdin in an adopted land. We kept the Lion Dance, and the Dragon Dance at the end.'

For the Tokyo production, Bintley and Davis revised and extended a Tchaikovsky-style divertissement called 'The Cave of Riches', based around the treasures that Aladdin discovers there. They started with a *pas de six* representing the least valuable jewels – onyx and pearls – and gradually reduced the dancers down, five girls representing the sapphires; a quartet for gold and silver; a trio for emeralds; a duet for rubies, until the most valuable of the jewels, diamonds, is danced by a solo ballerina accompanied by the *corps de ballet*. The section for emeralds caused a few problems. 'Carl had decided that emeralds should represent envy,' says Bintley, 'so he had one of the dancers jealously emulating the girl who danced in the rubies duet. It was an envious take on another piece, and I couldn't see that it would work.'

'David told me that the one thing he didn't understand was my music for emeralds,' Davis explains. "I said that it would be like the *Carmen* prelude – it would be about envy, which is associated with the colour green. It was about a jealous woman. David didn't get that, so I rewrote it as an oriental, Indian-influenced, jungle scene instead.'

Davis says he was doubly honoured when David Bintley presented a new production of *Aladdin* in 2013 with his Birmingham Royal Ballet, including a London season. The production was remounted in 2014 by the Houston Ballet in Texas, USA, and there are plans for further revivals in Japan and the UK.

'I think that Carl would be happiest if he was working on a ballet every single day of his life,' says Bintley. 'That is really what brings him alive. Over the past forty years he has written dance music for practically every ballet company in the country, and many of his pieces have lasted. He has this special quality of not only having great knowledge of the ballet world, but also a great love of it. He has the ability to capture a mood and a place, which to a certain extent twins with his work for film and TV. As soon as he has an extraneous idea that fires his imagination, then the sound-world comes with it, and music, dance and the idea itself all coalesce. That's a special gift, a different proposition from other composers who work mostly in non-theatrical musical genres, who may or may not be capable of writing a terrific ballet. If you know that that's what you're getting from Carl, he is absolutely the go-to person.'

VIII

CONCERT WORKS

Paul McCartney's Liverpool Oratorio

28 June 1991. Liverpool's Anglican Cathedral is packed out with an expectant audience. The front rows glitter with a welter of mayoral chains. The world's press is in attendance, cameras poised. The audience applauds as a quartet of internationally renowned soloists – Dame Kiri Te Kanawa, Sally Burgess, Jerry Hadley and Willard White – take their places in front of the Royal Liverpool Philharmonic Orchestra. Carl Davis steps on to the rostrum to conduct the eagerly anticipated premiere of the *Liverpool Oratorio*, Paul McCartney's first foray into the medium of classical music. He raises his baton – and, as if on cue, the vast space is plunged into darkness. There is an appalled silence as the audience holds its breath. Davis raises his fists to Heaven in furious supplication. He turns to the audience, saying: 'I think we would appreciate performing this work in some light!' A ripple of laughter dissipates the tension. In the darkness, technicians frantically work to fix the generators, and to everyone's relief the lights eventually come back on. 'I was really afraid that the mood would have been broken,' recalls Davis. 'I thought things might fall apart, but happily they didn't.'

As the performance ends, Paul McCartney runs down the central aisle, gives Davis a football salute, and the two men turn to acknowledge the applause, almost blinded by a battery of flashlights. 'I thought, this is the picture that will go round the world,' says Davis. 'And sure enough, when I flew to Montpellier the next day to conduct *Ben-Hur* at the Roman Arena in Nîmes, that picture was on the front page of the local paper.'

During the later 1980s, Carl's wife Jean had been starring in Carla Lane's enormously popular TV sitcom *Bread*, set in a poor working-class district of Liverpool, and dealing with a large and impecunious Catholic family, headed by Jean's character, matriarch Nellie Boswell. Carl got to know Carla Lane well. She was noted for her devotion to animals, and in 1988 she and Carl decided to collaborate on a group of three anthropomorphic concert works for Jean to narrate with orchestra, in the style of *Peter and the Wolf*. The first of these was *The Pigeon's Progress*. On the evening of its premiere, Carl bumped into the RLPO's programme director, coincidentally named Brian Pidgeon. Pidgeon said he wanted to discuss the fact that in 1991 the orchestra would be celebrating its 150th anniversary, and they wanted to commission a special piece to be performed in the Anglican Cathedral. On the spur of the moment, Davis suggested something by Paul McCartney, who was, after all, the most successful living Liverpool composer. Brian Pidgeon was delighted with the idea, and Davis was able to make contact with McCartney through Carla Lane. 'I remembered that Paul and Linda had actually appeared in an episode of *Bread*, and Jean had worked with them. So the message got to them via Carla, and I was invited to meet Paul at a house-party at their home.'

Composing a large-scale work for orchestra, soloists and chorus was clearly uncharted territory for McCartney, but Davis's extensive work in film and TV, together with the fact that he was a committed Beatles fan, made him an ideal collaborator. 'Paul and I discussed the broad outline of a piece sitting around the McCartney kitchen table. We decided it should be roughly autobiographical, based around incidents from Paul's early life. He started developing ideas – about the cathedral, and its ancient graveyard, his birth during the war, his schooldays, the death of his father.' Those ideas formed the basis of the first five sections of the oratorio, while the second part concerned the hero's meeting with and marriage to Mary Dee, and the birth of their first child. 'By the end of the first meeting, we had the germ of an idea. We were offered unlimited resources – a quartet of soloists, orchestra, chorus, the cathedral choir of boy trebles. But we had to resolve the question of division of roles. How we would evolve this was mysterious at first. I realised that Paul understood the mechanics of classical composition, but it needed to be organic – the joins mustn't show. I knew Paul was used to working closely with John Lennon and George Martin, among others, and I was confident that we could work something out. We evolved a collaborative *modus vivendi*. The piece took shape and began to have a story. It became almost operatic. I remember one particular confrontation between the soprano and the tenor, in which Paul conceived the text and the melody at the same time. When I'm writing vocal music, I approach it through the classical method – someone writes a text, and I set it. But this isn't how it happens in the pop world, where all the elements of a song evolve together. By the end of that session we were able to play the words, the vocal line and the accompaniment together. That was a red-letter day.'

As the project grew, the huge publicity machine surrounding McCartney became involved. TV and recording deals were struck. *Paul McCartney's Liverpool Oratorio* was to be recorded on CD for EMI, on DVD, and a separate documentary film was to be made about the creation of the piece. Davis and McCartney were trailed throughout the process. Then, shortly before the premiere, McCartney asked if he could hear a complete run-through of the performance. The glamorous soloists were unavailable, so a different batch had to be quickly hired and rehearsed, and the preview performance itself was filmed. One of Carl Davis's most amusing memories of the actual rehearsal for the premiere was overhearing Dame Kiri Te Kanawa saying urgently: 'I've got to find Jean! I must find Jean! I need to know how to say "I'm going to have a baby" in a Liverpool accent!'

The great day arrived. What no one had foreseen was that by then there were so many different media involved – the film of the documentary, the film of the actual performance, the equipment for the CD recording – all competing for a share of Liverpool

Cathedral's modest electricity supply. 'On the night before the show,' says Davis, 'the engineer who was supervising the CD recording, the late John Timperley, famous for his meticulous approach, said that there was a terrible hum from all the power trucks stationed outside. "What do you need to block this noise?" asked Paul. "Maybe some hay to pack the wall," said John. Paul clicked his fingers. "Get hay!" – and within an hour bales of hay arrived, to pack round the power unit. That sorted the hum, but at the actual performance, when all the power units were switched on at the same time, they blew the overloaded system.'

Despite its teething troubles, *Paul McCartney's Liverpool Oratorio* was deemed a success. It had over 100 performances in two years, and two songs from it, *The World You're Coming Into* and *Save the Child*, were released as singles in the autumn of 1991.

Compared with Carl Davis's extensive output in other categories, his catalogue of concert works is modest. In 1980 he composed a London Symphony – his first – at the request of Capital Radio. 'Capital Radio wanted something classical, as part of their remit then. The symphony had its premiere by the Wren Orchestra in June 1980, and was later played by the Royal Philharmonic Orchestra at the Festival Hall. There is a sort of No. 2, but definitely no No. 3.' Apart from many concert suites derived from his film scores, he has since written a handful of instrumental pieces, including a Clarinet Concerto, a Fantasy for flute, strings and harpsichord, and the Ballade for cello and orchestra (2011), written for the principal cello of the RLPO, Jonathan Aasgaard. 'I have composed works for the concert hall, but my principal compositions have been in film and TV. Because I am riveted by my sense of theatre, history, dance, I need a hook of some kind. I find it very difficult to work only with abstract ideas. My music is livelier if it has an extra motivation.'

Last Train to Tomorrow

One such motivation, threaded through Davis's work since the 1970s, is that of the suffering experienced by Europeans during the Second World War. The theme of the Holocaust provided the impetus for Davis's most important concert work in recent years, *Last Train to Tomorrow*, a cantata for children's choir and instrumental ensemble with spoken dialogue. It deals with the emotive subject of the wartime *Kindertransport*, a rescue operation for Jewish children initiated in the aftermath of *Kristallnacht* in November 1938. Alarmed by the increasing intensity of attacks on Jewish families in central Europe, a group of British Jews and Quakers petitioned the British Government to facilitate the evacuation and entry into Britain of imperilled unaccompanied Jewish children under the age of seventeen. As a result, around ten thousand children were evacuated by train from Berlin, Vienna and Prague in the months leading up to the outbreak of World War II in September 1939. Around 700 came from Prague, where Nicholas Winton, a young British stockbroker of German-Jewish origin, gave up his annual holiday to organise the evacuations, along with a few colleagues. Although the children who travelled on the evacuation trains themselves were saved from the Holocaust, the story is a traumatic one, as most never saw their families again. The final train organised by Winton, carrying some 250 children, was prevented from departing by the outbreak of war. Nearly all those on board eventually perished in Nazi death camps.

Carl Davis has always found the subject of this wartime rescue operation very moving. His wife Jean had had an important role in Diane Samuels's play, *Kindertransport,* which the Soho Theatre Company had produced at the Cockpit Theatre in London in April 1993, and which then transferred to the Strand, and ran for six months. Jean had played a Manchester mother who takes in one of the refugee children. Davis himself had friends who had been on the *Kindertransport*, including Edward Mendelson, who became a successful architect. Davis says: 'It's hard in the arts not to know someone who was involved. Some years ago I began working a lot in the Czech Republic, and one day, while I was doing a concert in a city in the eastern part of the country called Ostrava, I had a phone call from the state TV of that area. They were making a documentary about Karel Reisz, who had been born there, and they wanted to interview me about working with him.' (Davis had worked with Reisz in 1981 on *The French Lieutenant's Woman*.) 'In the course of that interview, I found out that he had been on the *Kindertransport*. Like a lot of his fellow refugees, he never talked about it. It had been too traumatic. And from my work with the Royal Liverpool Philharmonic, I knew Lady Milina Grenfell-Baines, who organised the orchestra's concert series in Preston. She had originally come from Prague as a child on the *Kindertransport*.'

In 2012, Davis was asked by John Summers, the CEO of the Hallé Orchestra, if he might like to write a piece for the Hallé Children's Choir. The orchestra is very proud of its choir, and each year commissions a new piece for them. Davis jumped at the chance. 'I love to write for chorus, and that is a virtuoso children's choir. Then I thought about the story of the *Kindertransport*. I realised I would like to tell the story. It would be different and exciting. This is a great story of English tolerance and open-heartedness that reaches out not just to the past, but to the present day as well. I also noticed that the choir stalls in the Bridgewater Hall could be said to resemble a railway carriage. The dimensions are similar – a long cylinder.'

Both John Summers and the choirmistress at the Hallé, Shirley Court, were enthusiastic about the idea, and Carl Davis approached Hiawyn Oram, with whom he had written children's musicals including *Vackees*. 'We decided to tell the story through a sequence of songs,' he says. 'I saw it as a latter-day *Winterreise*. The majority of the children were educated and musically literate, surrounded by classical music on the radio and gramophone, as well as home music making. We needed to convey some element of their backgrounds – they would have been brought up in the great Austro-German musical tradition. However I was anxious not to surround the children with gorgeous Wagnerian orchestration. I chose a simpler sound, of strings, piano (four hands) and percussion, the sort of austere scoring typical of much concert music written in the late 1930s, but not an unfriendly sound and one which would not overwhelm the children. If you use the traditional mix of winds, brass and strings, it's immediately colourful, rich and warm – all the things I didn't want in *The Last Train*, which is a tragic story with a flash of optimism.'

For the sake of continuity, Oram and Davis decided that there should be some spoken text, delivered initially by actors, who would represent the adults involved in the drama – parents, Red Cross nurses, SS officers – as well as the older children. For the original production, which took place at the Bridgewater Hall in Manchester on 17 June 2012, they used six third-year drama students from Manchester Metropolitan University. The actors stood at the front of the stage, re-enacting various events, while the children were placed behind the orchestra. The premiere was attended by many *Kindertransport* survivors, and proved a highly emotional occasion.

Davis conceived *Last Train to Tomorrow* as a journey from darkness into light. This is a specifically Jewish story, and his score draws on Jewish modal scales, with their characteristic flattened intervals, to underline the children's experience. The score is akin to a short musical, with occasional echoes of the style of *Fiddler on the Roof*. After a menacing Prelude, pregnant with foreboding, children's voices recount the humiliations heaped on them and their families – their mothers forced to scrub streets on their knees, their Aryan friends deserting them and throwing stones at their school bus, their eviction from cafés and parks. In 'Before This', the emigrating children count the passing stations through Czechoslovakia, Austria and Germany, while recalling happier days when they went fishing and swimming, and ate *Apfelstrudel* in cafés, before the arrival of the Nazi menace. Then comes the terror of *Kristallnacht* (Night of Breaking Glass), when Jewish businesses and synagogues were attacked and destroyed. Davis evokes the smashing and tinkling of broken glass in the Bartókian timbres of piano and percussion, against which fragments of Central European musical classics – Mozart's *Eine kleine Nachtmusik*, the *Blue Danube* Waltz, the Christmas carol *Stille Nacht* – are all brutally cut off with the word 'No!'

In 'Train Rumours', a tense, whirling waltz, clandestine rumours begin to circulate that Jewish children might be allowed out on special trains, so long as they have the right papers. 'A Big Adventure', set as recitative-like solos with chorus, describes the agony of parting at the station, where frantic parents exhort their children to be brave and cheerful. As 'The Journey Begins', the children are packed into railway carriages, half excited, half fearful, and keep their spirits up by singing the nostalgic Czech anthem 'Where is my homeland'. A violin solo introduces the jaunty, waltz-like 'A Ring in the Heel of a Shoe', in which the children describe how they have tried to hide small treasures – a watch, a ring – in their clothing, counterpointed with the recurrent chorus 'Crossing the border, crossing the line'.

The mood turns ugly as border guards rip the children's suitcases and clothes apart, depriving them of the few small valuables that they have been allowed to bring. 'Goodbye to our Treasures' is the last specifically Jewish-sounding number in the score, as a poignant cello solo underlines the children's sense of loss. But the trains reach the German border, and once across the Dutch frontier, the children experience 'Sudden Love and Kindness', as well-meaning adults offer them food and hot chocolate. Bitter experience has taught them to be wary, and the fragmented vocal line describes their psychological trauma. In the last musical number, 'Sun Rising on Another World', the modal, Central European musical idiom finally gives way to a brighter, more optimistic major key, as the weary travellers arrive safely on the English coast, and realise that 'Day will always follow night here'.

In 2013 *Last Train to Tomorrow* received its second performance in Prague, with the Children's Opera of Prague and members of the Czech National Symphony Orchestra, who subsequently recorded it in English. Then in 2014 the Association of Jewish Refugees in England sponsored a further performance at the Roundhouse, a converted former railway engine shed in Chalk Farm, north London – a perfect venue, both for its association with trains, and for its circular shape. That performance, by the Finchley Children's Choir and the City of London Sinfonia, took place on 9 November 2014, the 76th anniversary of *Kristall-nacht*. It was attended by Prince Charles, together with many *Kindertransport* survivors. Davis coupled *Last Train* with the Mendelssohn Violin Concerto, since Mendelssohn's music was banned during the Nazi period.

Another appropriate anniversary, National Holocaust Memorial Day on 27 January 2016, provided the impetus for the fourth performance of *Last Train to Tomorrow* in Chichester Cathedral, with the children from a local Church of England primary school dressed in appropriate 1930s costumes, standing in front of the orchestra. This was the first time the cantata had been performed in a specifically Christian building – a venue freighted with symbolism. And in 2017 it will be performed in a Jewish building – a refurbished synagogue in Maidenhead, the home-town of Sir Nicholas Winton, who died on 1 July 2015, aged 106.

Carl Davis regards *Last Train to Tomorrow* as a significant achievement. 'People are genuinely touched by it, so my music must have succeeded in capturing the right tone. There are moments when I have thought: "Am I right to be doing this, to make people who have undergone such terrible experiences, and are still emotionally so raw, confront and relive their trauma?" But the story has to be told, it must be remembered, because history keeps repeating itself. Nevertheless the raw human emotion is very jarring. The audiences for that piece will include relatives of people who went through it, and even survivors themselves – sometimes when I meet members of the audience afterwards a man might shake my hand, and then lift his sleeve – and there is a tattoo. You are holding the hand of someone who has suffered. That's tough – I don't know how I could ever become hardened to that. But I elected to do it.'

CODA: INTO THE FUTURE

In 2003 the British Academy of Film and Television Arts honoured Carl Davis with a Special Lifetime Achievements Award for his contribution to the worlds of film and television, and two years later he was made a CBE. Both his parents were present when he was the subject of Thames Television's celebrity guest show *This Is Your Life* in 1986: his father died in 1990, while his mother, who had moved to Florida to join other family members, lived to celebrate her hundredth birthday in 2010. Six years later, as Carl Davis reaches his own eightieth birthday, his prodigious energy and appetite for work remains undiminished. He and Jean have lived in a succession of large, sprawling houses in Streatham, Barnes and Chelsea, and their current home, a grand, red-brick Georgian house in the centre of Windsor, is a hive of frenetic activity. Carl uses different rooms, ranging from his book- and score-lined study to desks in bedrooms, to accommodate individual projects in separate areas. He still sketches all his music out by hand on manuscript paper, while his assistant James works at an editing suite in a cottage over the old coachhouse. Both Victoria, his PA, and his daughter Jessie, who deals with rights issues, have offices in the main house. Jean's realm is the comfortable family kitchen and adjoining snug, while the household is ruled in queenly fashion by Diva the plump dachshund.

Davis is currently at work on several projects simultaneously – completing his score for Rudolph Valentino's swansong, *The Son of the Sheik* for release on DVD and Blu-Ray; creating new ones for Harold Lloyd and Buster Keaton films; contemplating another ballet, and working on his first animated film, Raymond Briggs's *Ethel and Ernest*. The film, which stars the voices of Jim Broadbent and Brenda Blethyn as Raymond Briggs's parents, and Luke Treadaway as Raymond himself, is produced by Camilla Deakin and Ruth Fielding, and directed by Roger Mainwood. It will be shown on the BBC and in cinemas.

'This is a new way of working for me,' he says. 'Animated films are built up from layers: a simple pencil drawing will become charcoal, then gradually layered until eventually we have scenes as close to Briggs's original colours as possible. I have to be faithful to the subject, and the tone of the original. It's the story of Raymond's parents, from their meeting in 1928 to their deaths in the 1970s. Raymond is born halfway through. This working-class couple are frozen in their environment – they don't emerge from their South London home a great deal. The movement through the various epochs gives me a chance to reflect that in the music, from twenties and thirties jazz through the war years, the light music of the fifties, then the pop and rock of the sixties. My score will be punctuated by original music of the various periods.

'*Ethel and Ernest* is one of the hardest projects I've had to do, and initially gave me quite some difficulty. I succeeded in composing a title-theme, which will become the film's principal theme, almost immediately, but the problem is to match the specific tone of Raymond Briggs. That has proved very hard. Briggs's book has a simplicity, but at the same time it's very guileful, very clever. The central couple's relationship is fascinating. It seems simple, but it's actually far from straightforward, and it has to support a certain level of comedy. It's very "English" – understated, but it packs a powerful punch. Pitching it right is difficult for me, since I'm used to working on a big emotional canvas. I need to go back to a *Pride and Prejudice* mode, another story which dealt with human emotions on a relatively small scale, but also could see the comic side of life.

'You need experience to learn how to find exactly the right solution. The material is exposed now – I've got my themes, and I know what brings a smile to my colleagues' faces.'

In addition, Carl is adding assiduously to his personal recording catalogue, *The Carl Davis Collection*. 'I always recognised the importance of recording my work, so that the music is permanently at your disposal. It's part of my history and part of our business. Being in the commercial world has a terrific excitement and meaning. I made my first recording back in the 1960s, when I met Fenella Fielding while I was working on *Diversions* and on curtain music for a West End farce called *Big Bad Mouse*. Fenella had a beautiful sexy voice, so I said: "We'll write a song and record it." She obliged. It was a Charleston-like number, it did very well, and was played on the radio. Then when I was working on Alan Bennett's *40 Years On*, I started a collaboration with George Fenton, who acted in the play. We wrote some songs based on themes thrown up by the play, and got them released.'

In the late 1970s, Davis signed a contract with Terry Oates, the director of Eaton Music. Oates concluded a three-record deal with EMI for some of Davis's film and TV music over the next few years, including *The Last Night of the Poms*, and music from the *Hollywood* series. Shortly afterwards, more of Davis's music appeared on disc, including an LP of extracts from *Napoléon*, and the *Champions* title-music. But during the recessionary years of the late 1980s and '90s, record companies began to retrench and withdraw from contracts. Record shops closed with the advent of digital, the once booming CD market began to shrink, customers' preferences altered, and the recording industry changed immeasurably.

As the new millennium dawned, Carl Davis began to feel frustrated. 'I felt I would like to be more in control of my recording projects, to control my own rights, and to be able to collect royalties. The collection societies – PRS and MCPS – are so important to a composer. By the mid-2000s Jean and I felt we had outlived life in Chelsea, so in 2009 we sold the London house and moved out to Windsor, to be nearer Jessie and our three grandchildren. We used the capital from the sale of the house to form a record company, with myself, Jean and Jessie as directors.

We wanted to be able to issue recordings springing from my concert work – a Bond CD, a Beatles CD, an ABBA CD, and so on, as well as extracts from my film music – 'Carl's War', extracts from *The World at War*, and so on. In 2014 we issued the CD of the Czech recording of *Last Train to Tomorrow*, and in 2016 we will issue a CD and DVD of the digitally restored version of *Napoléon*. I have also financed the release on DVD of Chaplin's *Mutuals*, re-edited in a new edition by the BFI, and we are licensing films for which I composed music.

'I have enormous ambitions for *The Carl Davis Collection*, which currently comprises about thirty discs and is growing fast. We have moved into the digital age, and are now selling online. Also, part of any conductor's profession is to record well. The studio is an arena in which you are performing.'

Carl Davis remains at heart a true performer. 'There are moments when I'm conducting something that makes me feel "it can't get any better than this". I had that sensation when I conducted *Giselle* with English National Ballet, with two wonderful Estonian dancers in the central roles. I had only conducted some of my own ballet music before, never anyone else's, and as these performances progressed, they just got better and better, and so did my conducting. It's the same with certain moments of synchronisation in live performances of the silent films. For instance, there's a particular moment when I'm aiming for a climactic point in Buster Keaton's *The General*. He's on a train, and the people who have kidnapped his locomotive have strewn logs on the line. Buster realises that he can save the train by treating the logs like pick-up sticks, and I've arranged the score so that the music builds and builds until the moment when he flings the logs aside. If I can time my synchronisation so that it hits the climactic chord at the precise moment when he drops a log, the audience is delighted at Keaton's ingenuity, and simply explodes.

'It's those moments of empathy with an audience that are so precious. Getting a laugh is a great thrill. I learned that when I was working with Barry Humphries. That power of comic timing, so that the audience roars, is endlessly fascinating. It's the same with dressing up for concerts. I'll never forget the audience's reaction when I first walked out wearing a British Railwayman's cap to conduct the Royal Liverpool Philharmonic Orchestra. You walk out on stage and people roar. You have asked for that laugh, and got it.'

In the realms of film and TV music, Carl Davis's work has blazed a trail over the past half-century, with others now following in his footsteps. 'To musicians of my generation,' says the highly successful film and TV composer Howard Goodall, 'Carl has been a beacon of integrity, inventiveness and professionalism, and I salute him with enormous admiration and respect.'

'Looking back over my own work,' says Davis, 'I think I am most proud of my music for *The World at War*, which was so effective in the studio. And my scores for *Pride and Prejudice* and *The French Lieutenant's Woman* seemed to encapsulate the moods and the subjects.'

'Carl is a major figure in British TV history,' says Jeremy Isaacs. 'His importance cannot be exaggerated, particularly with regard to *The World at War*, *Hollywood* and, above all, to the seasons of silent movies.'

'Without Carl Davis, Live Cinema would never have happened,' says Kevin Brownlow. Neil Brand, a silent-film accompanist and composer of scores for silent films, concurs. 'Carl drew the whole nation's attention to the music for silent film. We in the industry owe him a huge debt, but so does anybody with an interest in culture and an art form that he has done so much to revive and celebrate.'

In Kevin Brownlow's opinion, Carl Davis is by far the finest composer in this area. 'One of the worst things to hit silent film in the last twenty years is totally unsympathetic musical accompaniment. The greatest silent German film, *Variety*, a masterly film, has finally been released in a superb restoration. They have given it a soundtrack by a group called the Tiger Lilies. When it was premiered at the Venice Film Biennale, everyone complained about the music. It is simply awful. Gance's great pacifist masterpiece *J'accuse* has come out accompanied by an electric guitar! The only word to describe this is stupidity. The people who are making these decisions are just chasing a mythical "youth" audience, but all they are doing is alienating the audience they already have. It's rather like Muzak in a traditional restaurant. I just wish Carl could do all of them.'

'In Live Cinema,' says Davis, 'we established a way to reveal the silent movies at their best, accompanied by a live orchestra. The comedies are clever – *Safety Last* and *The General* are wonderful films. Films like *The Wind* or *The Crowd* are not popular films, but they are about the human heart, the human experience. And Von Stroheim's films – *Greed*, *The Wedding March* – their knowledge of human behaviour is so subtle, ingenious and fascinating. They were terrific things to do. But from a personal point of view I think the most fun for me as a composer are the romantic films, especially the Garbo films. They suit my mood and my character. I'm a romantic person, I believe in love. It's a great emotional work-out for me.'

And where does Abel Gance's great epic sit in Davis's personal pantheon?

'I don't regard my score for *Napoléon* as my greatest achievement. It's an extraordinary film, a massive film, and there are certainly spectacular things in it. I started with the most demanding project because of its length and the complexity of its story, and I relished the music, but I don't know how I did it, or how I got away with it.

'But I am very proud that I have been able, with Jean's help, to support the new recording. We first recorded *Napoléon* in 1983, when the film was still in its 1980 version. Since then Kevin Brownlow has picked up additional material, and was given access to Gance's original shot order. Kevin realised that some sections were in the wrong order, and so we had only had a partial view of it. He produced a second version, and then another restoration in 2000, which is the version that we have just recorded for release on DVD and Blu-Ray. The film now runs for about five and a half hours, and we feel that we are doing it in as definitive a version as possible, with a digitally improved and enhanced print. Gance himself never made a final complete version: after the premiere in 1927 he found himself historically out of step, as the film world was moving on and *Napoléon* had no soundtrack. He never really recovered, either artistically or professionally. If any more of the film turns up, I would naturally be delighted to work on it, but in terms of length it is already unwieldy, and practically impossible to put on for reasons of cost, even with new techno equipment available that means you no longer need the expense of four projectors. But I feel we have completed our statement. For me a chapter has closed.'

As ever, with Carl Davis, as one chapter closes, another will open. Everyone who has worked with him agrees that he is an unstoppable force of nature. 'I love what Carl does,' says the TV producer Sue Birtwistle. 'He is so wonderfully enthusiastic, it is totally captivating. I can't think of anything more fun than working on music with Carl – it's just paradise.'

'He has such an incurable interest and tremendous enthusiasm for things,' says the choreographer David Bintley. 'He collects everything that pertains to what he is working on and gathers it to him, so he is immersed in it. The passion! He doesn't do anything half-heartedly. But above and beyond all of his scores, he is Carl.'

'Working with Carl was a very big part of my life as a composer, and I feel very privileged to have been part of it,' says Colin Matthews. 'Carl is a cause worth celebrating.'

ACKNOWLEDGEMENTS

Many thanks to Carl and Jean for their warm and generous hospitality; to Victoria and Jessie for their unfailing helpfulness; to Sir Jeremy Isaacs, Sue Birtwistle, Colin Matthews, David Matthews, Kevin Brownlow and David Bintley for giving up their time to talk about their work with Carl; and to Lesley Rutherford, Sally Cavender and Richard King at Faber Music for all their help.

Wendy Thompson
October 2016

INDEX